SPIRAL GUIDE

MALLORCA

D0507276

AA Publishing

Contents

Written by Carol Baker
Magazine section by Teresa Fisher
Additional research by Mona King
Copy edited by Lodestone Publishing
Page layout by Design 23 and Jo Tapper
Index by Marie Lorimer
Updated by Tony Kelly
Update managed by Lodestone Publishing Limited

Published by AA Publishing, a trading name of Automobile
Association Developments Limited, whose registered office is
Millstream, Maidenhead Road, Windsor, Berkshire SL4 5GD.
Registered number 1878835.

ISBN 0 7495 2844 3

The contents of this publication are believed correct at the time of
printing. Nevertheless, AA Publishing accept no responsibility for any
errors or omissions or for changes in the details given in this guide or
for the consequences of readers' reliance on this information. This
does not affect your statutory rights. Assessments of attractions,
hotels, restaurants and so forth are based on the author's own experience and contain subjective opinions that may not reflect the
publishers' opinion or a reader's experience. We have tried to ensure
accuracy, but things do change so please let us know if you have any
comments or corrections.

A CIP catalogue record for this book is available from
the British Library

Reprinted 2003, Information verified and updated.
© Automobile Association Developments Limited 2001, 2003
Maps © Automobile Association Developments Limited 2001, 2003

Colour separation by Leo Reprographics
Printed and bound in China by Leo Paper Products

Find out more about AA Publishing and the wide range of travel
publications and services the AA provides by visiting our website at
www.theAA.com.

A01561

Mallorca

the magazine

A Chequered HISTORY

Mallorca has always been subject to foreign invasions, mainly because of its strategic geographical situation at the heart of the western Mediterranean. Civilisations from the Phoenicians to the tourists of today have left their mark on the physical and cultural landscape of the island, and have made it the epitome of Mediterranean insular history.

The first invaders were the Phoenicians, maritime traders from the eastern Mediterranean, around 1000 BC, followed by the Greeks who controlled the island for several centuries and gave the Balearic Islands their name, from *ballein* meaning "to throw from a sling", after the deft sling-shot throwers who fought as mercenaries in the Punic Wars of the 2nd and 3rd centuries BC.

The Balearics prospered for five peaceful centuries under the Romans, who introduced wine and olives to Mallorca, constructed cities at Pollentia (now Alcúdia) and Palmaria (modern-day Palma) and introduced Christianity. Following further conquests by Vandals and Byzantines in the 5th and 6th centuries, the island then suffered a period of devastating attack from the Muslim Moors.

The islanders put up a fierce struggle against the Moors until 902 when, with an armada of 300 ships, they were eventually outnumbered. But life under Moorish rule was not all bad: they introduced oranges, almonds and apricots, windmills and irrigation techniques, and Palma (then called

Medina Mayurqa) became a highly sophisticated capital with heated baths, streetlights and covered sewers. Word soon spread of this luxurious city, putting Mallorca at the top of the conquest list of Jaume I of Aragón, the young Catalan king who decided to wage war on the "unbelievers" and to capture the island.

For most Mallorcans, the history of their island only really began on 12 September, 1229 – the day Jaume I landed at Sa Caleta with 150 ships, 16,000 *conquistadores* and 1,500 horses. The Moors eventually capitulated and on 1 January, 1230, Jaume established himself in Palma ("the most beautiful city I have set eyes upon") – replacing mosques with churches, building Castell de Bellver (➤ 53–4) and converting the old Arab palace into a Gothic fortress. With Christianity soon re-established, the Kingdom of Mallorca gained power and importance, becoming one of the most dynamic and economically successful societies in Christendom, in the forefront of maritime trade and the quest for new colonies.

Centuries later, during the Spanish Civil War (1936–9), the development of this long-suffering island faltered once again, and the Franco era

Left: King Jaume I brought prosperity to the island
Right: Tiles at the Town Hall in Calvià
Page 5: Picturesque Cala Figuera

The Tourist Invasion

MALLORCA

Palma

(1939–75) brought repression throughout Spain. Franco banned the use of the local Catalan language and regional dialects, and all expressions of non-Castilian culture were suppressed. The end of the Franco era brought more security to the island, but little peace for it was in for another invasion – tourism. As a result of the new airborne crowds of package holiday-makers, the numbers of visitors increased rapidly, reaching a peak of over 8 million by the late 1990s. The desire to capitalise on this massive injection of cash led to some serious mistakes being made as giant concrete, tower-block hotels sprang up in vast, ugly tourist enclaves, ruining much of the island's coastline. Thankfully, these errors have since been recognised, and the islanders are working hard to preserve the character and appearance of Mallorca in the aftermath of one of the most destructive invasions in the island's history. Who knows…perhaps future historians will look back at the *turismo* period of the late-20th century and see it as just another phase in the island's rich history, and the strings of beach hotels fringing the coastline today as the monuments it has left behind.

Piracy

Mallorca has suffered centuries of piracy – as early as the 13th century, Jaume I described it as a "pirates' nest". One of the Balearics' most notorious pirates, Redbeard, had his base camp on the rocky island of Sa Dragonera, just 1km off the western tip of Mallorca, and in the 16th century, the islanders were forced to build their towns and villages (Andratx, Santanyí, Valldemossa) inland, away from their harbours as a precaution against pirate attack. Even today, pirates abound on Mallorca, but only in Magaluf, where "Pirates" offers fun-for-all-the-family theme nights of swashbuckling action, audience participation, and free-flowing Buccaneer's punch to loosen your inhibitions!

Unbeknown to most seaside holiday-makers, Mallorca is one of the finest bird-watching locations in Europe attracting "twitchers" from all over the globe. But why Mallorca? Not only is it located in a prime position for migrating birds to land each spring and autumn, but it also boasts a staggering diversity of habitats – marshes, reedbeds, fresh water lagoons, saltpans, scrubland, fields, orchards, woods, rocky sea cliffs and wild mountains.

The **golden rule** for bird-watching in Mallorca is: get up early! After about noon (11 am in summer) the island appears strangely birdless, but take a stroll in the countryside before breakfast and you will hear Sardinian warblers chirruping in the hedges, the chattering of woodchat shrikes, and the zip-zip call of tiny fan-tailed warblers. You may even glimpse a hoopoe, among the most striking birds on the island, with its striped wings and Native American chief's head-dress, flapping around the stone walls like a giant butterfly.

Rule two: look up! Even when you're basking in the sunshine, it's worth listening out for the occasional chirruping in the sky. There's no need even to move. Just open one eye and maybe you'll see a flock of swifts overhead, the dapper black-and-white Sardinian warbler delivering his rattling song from the tangled vegetation,

Above: The colourful bee-eater breeds in Mallorca in May
Below: A migrant woodchat shrike

Below: Redstarts migrate to Mallorca for the winter

BIRD WATCHING

or a swirl of bee-eaters, which appear black in silhouette but burst into all the colours of the rainbow if you are lucky enough to track them with binoculars.

Rule three: choose your season carefully. The island boasts abundant birdlife all year round but spring is the best time to visit. The island is packed with birds – residents, those visiting to breed and, best of all, it's migration time, with more than 200 species of birds on the move.

Rule four: know where to look! The best areas to head for with your binoculars and bird books are the remote, people-free parts of Mallorca. The **Bóquer Valley** (▶ 159) – a gap through the mountains north of Port de Pollença – is

the place to see migrants in springtime – in particular redstarts with their flashy red tails, pied flycatchers, and firecrests with their stripy heads and yellow jackets.

The rocky sea cliffs of nearby **Formentor** (▶ 99–100) are home to blue rock thrushes, chubby, small crag martins, and some of the rarest birds of the islands – Eleonora's falcons, booted eagles and red kites, which can occasionally be spotted swooping around the crags

Top: March is the best time to hear the song of the hoopoe
Above: Marsh harriers live in the wetlands around Pollença and Alcúdia

near Formentor lighthouse. You may even catch a glimpse here (or in the mountains) of the mighty black eagle, one of Europe's most endangered species. Also scan the sea far below for black storks patrolling the shoreline, or an osprey plunging down to catch its lunch.

Keen birdwatchers head straight to **S'Albufera** (▶ 165–7) – a Mediterranean fen, protected *Parc Natural* and the most important birdwatching site in the Balearics, with over 200 species of birds within a vast area of marshes, reedbeds and waterways. Here bitterns thrive and marsh harriers sail over the reedbeds which conceal herons and egrets, wildfowl dozing in the creeks, and elegant black-winged stilts, probing around the muddy lagoons.

Finally: keep your eyes peeled, even in seaside resorts. Stroll along the deserted beach at dawn or dusk to see a huge variety of gulls and waders strutting in the sand and shallows. During pleasure-boat rides, look out for graceful shearwaters, their wings virtually skimming the water in flight and, for the best seaboat twitching, be sure to tour the islands of Sa Dragonera or the National Park island of Cabrera, where 64 different seabird species have been spotted during spring migration.

Birdwatchers come to Mallorca all year round

The Threat of Tourism

As a result of mass tourism, the natural habitats and wildlife of Mallorca are under continual threat. Fortunately, through the recent efforts of the environmental group Grupo Ornitología Balear (GOB) and the local authorities, various species (including the black vulture and purple swamp hen) have been reintroduced to the island from mainland Spain, and almost one-third of the island is now protected in some way, ensuring its future as a paradise for birds and birdwatchers alike.

HOLA! Mallorca

Celebrity visitors past and present

M allorca has many strong associations with "celebrity" women. Some arrive in luxury yachts and cruise-liners; others rent villas high up in the mountains; while others stay in top hotels like the Son Vida (a favourite of the late Diana, Princess of Wales), Hotel Formentor and La Residencia, the grand hotel in Deià formerly owned by Sir Richard Branson's Virgin Group.

Deià boasts several famous female residents: surprisingly, perhaps, the first Mrs Branson lives here (an American called Kristen, who set up La Residencia with her second husband), as does Mrs Beryl Graves, the widow of writer Robert Graves (1895–1985), who still lives in the family home near the village graveyard where her husband is buried (➤ 91). Also in the village, you will find the home of British PR guru, Lynne Franks.

Two particularly popular female celebrities include British rock star Annie Lennox who has a property at Esporles in Mallorca's beguiling interior, while

supermodel Claudia Schiffer chose a luxury apartment by the sea at the stylish resort of Camp de Mar. German punk singer, Nina Hagen, lives on the island too.

Many who don't buy, enjoy holidays here: French novelist George Sand (1804–76)

Right: Catherine Zeta Jones stays near Deià

Claudia Schiffer is a regular visitor to the island

stayed at Valldemossa with Frédéric Chopin in the winter of 1838–9; British author Dame Agatha Christie (1890–1976) was a regular guest at Hotel Formentor, the first luxury hotel on the island, which opened in 1929 (she even set a story in nearby Pollença Bay), as was American actress Grace Kelly who later, as Princess Grace of Monaco, was a guest at the Son Vida Hotel's 1961 inauguration. More recently, American comedienne Ruby Wax has been a frequent guest at La Residencia, and

A Royal Residence

Both the Spanish and the British royal families frequently holiday here. King Juan Carlos and Queen Sofía (pictured left) of Spain spend the month of August in Mallorca's Royal Palace – Palau Marivent, overlooking Palma's yacht harbour on the fringes of Cala Major. They can frequently be seen sailing around the island on the Royal Yacht *Fortuna*, and competing in regattas such as the King's Cup and Princess Sofía Cup sailing events over Easter, while Princess Elena takes part in show-jumping competitions on the island, including the Princess Elena Horse Jumping Trophy in Bunyola in August. One of the patrons of the annual Sunseeker Celebrity Golf Classic tournament at Bendinat Golf Course in June is Princess Brigitta of Sweden, a keen golfer herself and captain of one of the 11 participating teams.

Celebrity Spotting

Where best to see famous faces:
Hotels: Son Vida, Hotel Formentor, La Residencia, Palacio Ca Sa Galesa.
Marinas: Portals Nous, Camp de Mar, Port d'Andratx.
Restaurants and Bars: Peppone Italian restaurant, Shangri-La Chinese and Mediterraneo 1930 restaurants and Abaco bar in Palma; Wellie's, Latino and Michelin-starred Tristans in Portals Nous.
Night-clubs: Pachá in Palma.

Two British actresses have graced Mallorca's shores: Patsy Kensit revealed her pregnancy to the world's press here, and Catherine Zeta Jones and her husband, American actor Michael Douglas, have a grand villa at Finca s'Estaca.

Mallorca's celebrities are no different from those anywhere else in the world but, because of the island's size, they are perhaps more noticeable. The islanders are flattered every time a star is so charmed by the island that, with the whole world to choose from, he or she buys property here.

What's more, celebrity women do, of course, attract the media, so their presence is applauded by many proud locals who see it as free publicity for their beloved island.

Rock star Annie Lennox, above left, snapped by the paparazzi in her pool

MALLORCAN
MONASTERIES

"It would be impossible to describe this gift from heaven. It is the most beautiful place that one could ever find in life", wrote French novelist George Sand in 1838 about the small hillside town of Valldemossa (► 88–90). She spent three months with her lover Frédéric Chopin staying in a small suite of monks' cells at the former Carthusian monastery, **La Reial Cartoixa**.

Their brief visit set a precedent for staying in the island's monasteries (sadly no longer possible at La Reial Cartoixa). Although most of the monks have since left, the religious orders continue their tradition of offering simple hospitality to pilgrims and travellers. Prices are low, facilities are basic – no mini-bar, air-conditioning or nightly chocolates on the pillow – but if you're hoping to

discover *la oltra Mallorca* (the other Mallorca), stay in one of the island's mountaintop monasteries. Built on the summits of peaks to escape the unwanted attention of smugglers and pirates, as well as to be nearer to God, the monasteries offer spectacular views and seclusion.

Near Palma airport, the revered **Puig de Randa** mountain rises abruptly out of the apricot orchards of the plain. At its summit, Mallorca's greatest son, 13th-century mystic and scholar Ramón Llull (► 147) established the island's first hermitage to atone for his life of excess, and spent ten years here in seclusion writing scholarly treatises. Today, pilgrims are as likely to be weekend cyclists as seekers of religious truth. The rooms are basic, clean and comfortable, and the

Lluc Monastery has been the island's main place of pilgrimage since the 13th century

café-bar serves hearty *tapas* (➤ 17–19), accompanied by magical views over much of the island.

Hidden in the craggy Serra de Tramuntana mountains, Lluc (➤ 96–8) has been you'll hear are hymns sung by the famous blue-cassocked *Els Blavet* choristers at dusk.

A short drive away, **Puig de Maria** (Mary's Mountain) overlooks the atmospheric town of Pollença and

Try to visit the monastery at Randa for the Blessing of the Crops on the fourth Sunday after Easter

Mallorca's centre of pilgrimage since the 13th century when an Arab shepherd boy called Lluch (Lucas), newly converted to Christianity, discovered a dark wooden statue of the Virgin in the forest, and local villagers built a chapel to house it. Today, that chapel forms part of the old Augustinian **Monestir de Lluc**, a colossal ensemble of pink-tinged stone buildings, including 100 monks' cells, now used to accommodate visitors, predominantly mountain walkers. This is the most comfortable of the island monasteries (but still reasonably priced) – more like a simple hotel than a hermitage, with *en suite* bathrooms for every cell, and even a restaurant and a bar. You do, however, have to make your own bed! The loudest sound

Pollença Bay beyond. An hour's hike will take you to the 14th-century sanctuary, where the caretaker will send down a mule for your luggage and, if you're lucky, will rustle up a *tortilla* and a glass of local *vino*, to save you the long trek into town for dinner. What's more, there are even hot showers.

More remote still is the sanctuary of **Nostra Senyora del Refugio**. To reach it, you have to drive for 5km up a pot-holed track, then climb for a further hour up a vertiginous, zig-zagging stony path, past the lofty ruins of the once impregnable Castell d'Alaró to a tiny sanctuary, restaurant and *hostal* at the summit. There are many reasons not to stay here: it's a long trek, accommodation is spartan,

it's cold at night and there's no shower. But think of the rewards! Peace, solitude and a view to die for – the sparkling sea on three sides, the protective Mountains of the North Wind on the other, and the pancake-flat plain stretched out below. In the distance, you can just make out Palma shimmering in the haze, and the noisy, tourist-courting beach resorts of Palma Bay – "the other Mallorca", a world away from the monasteries, the ideal retreat for the world-weary and discerning visitor.

The Santuari Cura de Randa sits atop Puig de Randa
Inset: Lluc Monastery is more like a hotel than a hermitage

Booking Information

It is advisable to phone in advance to **reserve accommodation**:
   Santuari Cura de Randa (tel: 971 120260);
   Monestir de Lluc (tel: 971 517025);
   Santuari del Puig de Maria, Pollença (tel: 971 184132);
   Hostal Nostra Senyora del Refugio, Castell d'Alaró
   (tel: 971 182112)

What Are Tapas?

Tapas – Spanish-style fish, meat or vegetable hors d'oeuvres – provide the ideal opportunity not only to sample *la cuina Mallorquina* but also to mingle with the locals. Rather than tucking into a full meal in a restaurant every night, why not try a succession of *tapas* dishes instead? Visit just one bar or, following the custom of the *tapeo*, move from bar to bar and sample just one dish in each.

The term "*tapas*" is believed to originate from the habit of having a few nibbles with a drink before a meal, to *tapar el apetito* (literally "to put a lid on the appetite"), or from the little saucers (*tapas*) of free snacks that bartenders used to place over drinks when they served their regulars. Some bars still serve free *tapas* at the bar – but usually

A *tapas* crawl in Palma

Although most bars throughout the island serve *tapas*, Palma boasts a particularly lively *tapas* scene. Start your "crawl" at **Bar Bosch** (Plaça Rei Joan Carlos I 6), for years a legendary meeting-place, great for people-watching. Continue on to tiny, jam-packed **El Pilón** (Carrer Cifre, just off the Born), famous for its seafood *tapas*, then try trendy, modern **Bruselas** (Carrer S'Estanc 4, also off the Born). As you get nearer the seafront, don't miss **La Paloma** (Carrer dels Apuntadors 16) for *tapas* by candlelight, but save the best till last, ending up at **La Boveda** (Carrer Boteria 3), a lively restaurant lined with giant wine barrels, with the most popular *tapas* bar in town.

Tapas are a way of life in Spain

only a bowl of olives or some salted almonds.

Many bars display the *tapas* on the counter so you can order just by pointing, but make sure you ask for the right type of portion – either a *tapa* or a *ración*. *Raciónes* are larger, served with bread and usually enough for a light meal. If you have trouble choosing, try a *tapa combinada* – a mouthful of everything. *Tapas* dishes range from simple bowls of marinated olives to a tasty *tortilla española* (chunky Spanish omelette filled with potato and onion and served cold in

slices), *empanadas* (meat pies), *cocas* (small pizza-like snacks), snails and red peppers in olive oil.

Dishes such as *tumbet* (see panel), *callos* (tripe in a tomato and onion sauce), and *frit mallorquí* (a hearty fry-up of offal, potatoes, onions and tomatoes) – are classic examples of Mallorcan cuisine: wholesome, simple peasant fare, steeped in tradition and rooted in local ingredients, with generous, flavoursome portions. The most popular bar-snack of all is the simplest: *pa amb oli* – hunks of brown bread, drizzled in

You'll find a large variety of *tapas* on offer – from olives to snails

Recipe – Tumbet

Tumbet is often described as a Mallorcan *rata-touille*, but it is not really that similar. The vegetables are cooked separately, potatoes are included, the mixture is layered and topped with a tomato sauce.

(Serves 6–8)

4 large potatoes, peeled and par-boiled
6 courgettes, topped and tailed
2 or 3 red peppers, topped, tailed and deseeded
2 large aubergines, topped and tailed
Extra virgin olive oil
Sea salt and freshly ground black pepper to taste
500ml passata (or home-made tomato sauce)

• Slice all the vegetables, brush with oil, season lightly and lay on baking sheets.
• Cook in a hot oven (or under the grill) until tender. Peel the peppers after cooking.
• Starting with the potatoes, layer the vegetables in an earthenware dish, pour the tomato sauce over the top and put in a hot oven for 10 minutes.

Serve hot or cold with crusty bread.

olive oil, rubbed with garlic and over-ripe tomato then sprinkled with salt; simple but delicious.

Different varieties of sausage can often be seen hanging from the rafters of bars: try *sobrasada* (minced pork with hot red peppers), *botifarró* (cured pork with blood), and spicy *chorizo* from mainland Spain. And every bar has its *jamón serrano*, a whole cured ham, on display. Near the coast, fish dishes predominate from simple, grilled *sardinas* (sardines) and *musclos al vapor* (steamed mussels) to

calamares en su tinta – jet-black rings of squid stewed in its own ink, perhaps the strangest-looking dish you are likely to encounter but surprisingly tasty.

Touristic
RENAISSANCE

Mallorca has cleaned up its act. No longer a byword for cheap-and-nasty package tourism, the island is now in the final throes of a remarkable transformation. Many resorts have been smartened up, lager louts have been replaced by more discerning tourists and, as a result, Mallorca is now considered a sophisticated holiday destination. Mallorca was the first place to experience the uncontrolled growth of mass tourism in the 1950s, which made it the richest region of Spain. Ironically, now it is leading the way in looking beyond it, by examining the recent past for guidance to its future.

Tourism accounts for a staggering 90 per cent of the island's income, but talk today is of "green", "sustainable" or "eco-" tourism: a shift away from budget sun-sea-and-sand holidays towards sporting or

cultural holidays which can be taken any time of the year – a development mirrored elsewhere in Spain. Rather than allow the island to slide inexorably downmarket, the regional government spent the 1990s investing heavily in infrastructure to attract more discerning visitors. Coastal resorts have reached saturation point during summer but, even so, there are strict environmental laws to stop more hotels being built. Many of the monstrous, concrete hotels that blotted the landscape have been demolished and replaced with stylish, traditional Spanish-style hotels and apartments. The regional government is also concentrating on the long-term upgrading of existing hotels. In other words: the policy is geared towards improving quality, not increasing capacity.

"Blue Flag" Beaches

Mallorca has been working hard since the 1980s to improve its beaches, and the efforts are now starting to pay off. Blue Flags are awarded for safe, clean and well-kept beaches and, in 2000, 28 beaches and 6 *puertos deportivos* (marinas) made the grade: a result of unanimous effort over the years to clean the sea, sand and marinas in the Balearics, an archipelago closely linked with the environment and tourism.

As a result, Mallorca is no longer irretrievably associated with grotty hotels, ruined coastlines and beaches jam-packed with "*los hooligans*". Admittedly, it is still the main British and German tourist destination in Europe, and there are still a few short stretches of coastline, principally either side of Palma, with their seemingly uninterrupted chain of characterless

The perenially popular beaches around Cala Ratjada

mega-resorts, but the rest of the island remains miraculously Mallorcan – rustic, peaceful and leisurely, an island for all seasons, with temperatures which are always mild and scenery which is always beautiful, and the tourist authorities are striving hard to keep it that way.

Take the multimillion peseta revamp of Magaluf, for instance. It was once a cheap, brash holiday resort full of lager-fuelled *gamberros Ingleses* (English thugs) and their Continental equivalents, who wanted to get sunburnt

Agroturismo

One of the most popular tourism schemes on Mallorca is the new wave of *agroturismo*, with visitors flocking to stay in *fincas* (family-run farmhouses) in the hinterland. This back-to-nature approach offers the highly sought-after peace and tranquillity of the island, a valuable insight into the island's history and culture, *and* it suits the locals, many of whom can no longer afford to run their *fincas* solely from farming. At present, there are some 80 *agroturismo* properties on the island, with more opening all the time, each providing an opportunity to appreciate the richness of an island that has always been far more than a developer's playground. For details contact Agroturismo (➤ 34).

and drunk as inexpensively as possible. Today, although still popular with a young crowd, it is a stylish, elegant resort. Some of its ugly breeze-block high-rise hotels have been destroyed, the beach (now one of Mallorca's best) has been widened, and replenished with fine, golden sand, and a new and attractive palm-lined promenade has been added which has rejuvenated the beach-side cafés and restaurants and led to the opening of several smart, new waterfront enterprises.

Palma, too, has smartened up its image since the 1920s, shedding its dusty provincialism to become one of Europe's more fashionable cities – a paradise for sun-hungry visitors and a chic summer haunt for the rich and famous, stylish, sophisticated and teeming with life and atmosphere, a more intimate version of Barcelona with its café society and its flourishing arts scene.

A less-popular development, however, was the introduction of the tourist "eco-tax" in the summer of 2002, which raised the cost of a family holiday to the Balearics considerably. According to a poll in a local magazine, resident opinion is firmly behind the scheme, but it received a hostile reaction abroad

It Is too early to say whether the government has perhaps shot itself in the foot. It seems likely that the eco-tax will result in fewer people visiting Mallorca...but then, would that be such a bad thing?

Hotel swimming-pools (here, at Deià and Banyalbufar) offer a private and convenient alternative to the sea

Paradise Lost?

In a remarkably short period of time, tourism has made Mallorca the richest region of Spain. The sudden influx of package tourism in the 1950s came as a shock to this sleepy, sun-baked island. However, the residents were quick to catch on to the enormous economic potential of their beaches. Developers rushed in, bulldozing their way along the coast around Palma, in an uncontrolled building boom that changed the landscape and the economic and social structure of the island. Today tourism accounts for a staggering 90 per cent of the island's income.

MODERNISMO
THE EPOCH OF
BAD TASTE

Ironically, *Catalan modernismo* – the most distinctive style of Mallorcan architecture – owes its presence on the island to an orange blight in the 1860s in Sóller. The villagers were forced to emigrate to the far corners of Europe in search of work, returning at the turn of the 20th century, having made their fortune abroad. With this new-found wealth, they contracted the best of a new breed of radical Catalan architects to bring the latest European fashion to the island – *modernista* architecture, an ornate, often startling and surreal, Catalan variant of art nouveau. Thus begun a phase in Mallorcan building known to some as *la época de mal gusto* (the epoch of bad taste).

The first modernist building – the ornamental Gran Hotel (today the Fundació la Caixa, ► 58), designed by Lluis Domènech i Montaner – was constructed in Palma in 1902. At the same time, Palma's forward-looking Bishop Campíns, having seen the design for Gaudí's remarkable Sagrada Familia cathedral in Barcelona, invited the world-renowned Catalan architect to restore Palma's magnificent 14th-century cathedral.

Gaudí spent the next ten years on the project, helped by his student assistant Joan Rubió. They introduced electric lighting, ceramic inlays and wrought-iron railings inspired by Mallorquín window-grilles. But the most radical addition was the *Crown*

La Caixa features distinctive floral ornamentation

of Thorns, a dramatic canopy of cardboard, cork, brocade and nails, suspended above the altar. Although highly controversial at the time, today it is one of *the* sights of this magnificent cathedral.

Gaudí's presence influenced many of Palma's early 20th-century buildings, including Pensió Menorquina and Can Casasayas in Plaça del Mercat – their vivacious, rippling façades both decorated with

Prunera (Carrer Sa Lluna 90), now a private house.

Surprisingly however, it was neither Gaudí nor Rubió, nor any architect, but a silver-smith who left the most memorable legacy of modernism on the island. His name was Lluís Forteza Rei and his mansion, Can Forteza Rey in

Modernista details can be found throughout Mallorca

butterfly and fern motifs. He also worked on the church at Lluc (➤ 96), creating five striking sculptures to represent the *Mysteries of the Rosary* on the mountain behind the monastery complex, before suddenly abandoning the island for unknown reasons in 1914, leaving behind several unfinished projects.

Meanwhile, Rubió, his protégé, stayed on in Sóller, producing some of the finest examples of *modernista* architecture on the island, including the parish church and the Banco de Sóller, with its ornately twisted window-grilles. You can peek into the entrance hall of his home in Sóller, extravagant Can

Palma (Plaça Marquès del Palmer), with its colourful mosaic façade and ornate wrought-ironwork, has since become the eye-catching standard bearer of *modernista* architecture, a style which though regarded by many Mallorcans as extravagant and tasteless at the time, is today acknowledged as one of the greatest phases in the island's architectural history.

THE GOOD,

Beaches

The finest: The vast, sandy beaches of Magaluf and Palma Nova near by; palm-lined Platja Formentor with sand like icing-sugar.

Best for swimmers: The coves of Cala Sant Vicenç, each glistening with crystal-clear water.

Most crowded: Cala Millor.

Most exotic bar: Abaco, Palma's most unusual cocktail bar (Carrer Sant Joan 1) is situated inside a 17th-century mansion and decorated with caged birds, fountains and huge displays of fruit.

Most sophisticated night-life: Portals Nous is the St Tropez of the Balearics and

Below: Enjoying the fun at Aquacity in Arenal

THE

Most deserted: Cala Pi (south of Llucmajor); Cala de Deià.

Best water sports: Torrenova is great for fun activities – banana rides, jet-skiing, water-skiing, paragliding; Pollença Bay offers ideal conditions for learning to sail or windsurf.

Night-life

Worst night-out: The cabaret show at Son Amar unless, of course, you're into Spanish ballet, magicians, flying dancers and a live concert by The Drifters!

Best clubbing spots: Magaluf and Torrenova boast a number of top night haunts including the renowned Millennium discotheque, Carwash and Boomerangs. In Arenal, the giant RIU-Palace is one of Mallorca's best night-spots, while Alcúdia's biggest, most popular club, Menta, features an indoor swimming-pool.

Rowdiest resorts: Probably Torrenova and Arenal at closing time.

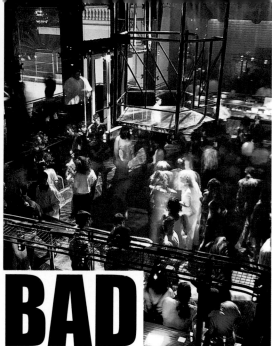

BAD AND THE UGLY

its glitzy marina, crammed with fashionable restaurants and bars, is a great venue for celebrity-spotting.

Resorts

Most photogenic resort: The tiny fishing village of Cala Figuera, near Santanyí, with fishermen's cottages and boathouses lining a narrow inlet.

Ugliest resort: The characterless resorts of Sa Coma and S'Illot are overflows of Cala Millor, and both merge in a seemingly endless row of ugly hotels. The sandy beach and mini-train are their saving grace.

Liveliest resort: It's still hard to beat Arenal, Magaluf and Torrenova for round-the-clock fun.

Hardest resort to park in: The parking is horrible at Illetas, but thankfully it has regular buses from the centre of Palma, and connections to all the other south-coast resorts.

Family fun

Best family resort: Palma Nova.

Best family entertainment. Aquacity in Arenal – the largest waterpark in Europe – also has go-karting, parrot shows, falconry demonstrations and a mini-farm to keep all the family amused.

Best family night-out: Pirates, a rip-roaring buccaneers' show, with audience participation.

Most family-oriented bar: Cheers (Avinguda Venecia) in Port d'Alcúdia, with a special kids' menu and entertainment all day long.

Shopping

Chicest shopping: Palma.

Best buys: Glass from Lafiore (showroom on the road to Valldemossa), wine from Binissalem, pearls from Manacor, leather from Inca.

Top markets: The leather market in Inca on Thursday mornings; the livestock market in Sineu for a taste of

Mallorca's best fiestas

(check with the local tourist office for exact dates)

May Moors and Christians: Sóller is "defended" against a "Moorish invasion" in a stirring re-creation of Mallorcan history (and a similar fiesta takes place in August in Pollença).

June Saint Peter: the patron of fishermen is honoured with processions of fishing boats in the island's ports.

July Fishermen's Festival: another procession of fishing boats, this time in honour of the Virgin Mary throughout the island.

August Cavallets: Felanitx's famous festival, in which children gallop about on papier-mâché hobby-horses, chased through the streets by *cabezudos* ("big heads" – traditional Spanish giants).

September Carro de la Beata: a showy fiesta with devils infiltrating a procession of villagers dressed in rural costume.

October Festa d'es Botifarró: the "Sausage Feast" at Sant Joan, marking the arrival of winter, is one of Mallorca's more eccentric fiestas.

rural island life; Palma's *baratillo* (flea market) on Saturday mornings (Avinguda Gabriel Alomar i Villalonga).

Sightseeing

Most tranquil Mallorca: Es Pla, the agricultural heartland of the island, with its sleepy country town and rural landscape dotted with windmills, orchards and apricot groves.

Most scenic Mallorca: The northwest coastline from Andratx to Deià; the Serra de Tramuntana; the cape of Formentor.

Most traditional Mallorca: La Granja, a fine country-house-cum-open-air-museum of rural life and traditions.

Prettiest village: Fornalutx, once voted the prettiest village in Spain.

Best day-trip: The "toytown" train from Palma to Sóller.

Most beautiful gardens: The cool, shady Moorish gardens of Alfàbia.

Most boring museum: Palma's Diocesan Museum, attached to the cathedral.

It is easy to see how Palma got its name

Opposite: The luxurious gardens of Alfàbia, which means "jar of olives" in Arabic

For a less Mallorcan experience, British-style food is available in nearly every resort

Did you Know?

• Spain is the second top destination for holiday-makers in Europe and Mallorca is the top destination in Spain. Latest tourism figures show that around 40 per cent of overnight stays in Spain are actually in Mallorca.

• **Mallorca's coastline is 555km long with a total of 179 beaches. Its longest beach – at Alcúdia – stretches for 12km, with fine, golden sand gently shelving into shallow water, the occasional beach bar and plenty of water sports facilities providing fun for all the family. It also flies the highest number of Blue Flags in Europe, with 28 beaches receiving this accolade in 2000.**

• In a late 1990s survey by Spanish newspaper *El País*, Palma was voted the best place to live in Spain – because of its sheer vitality, the flair and enthusiasm of its inhabitants, the chic shops and avant-garde galleries, the chatter of the tapas bars, the café society and the excellent restaurants which offer the best in Spanish, Catalan and Mallorcan cuisine.

• **Most Mallorcans are bilingual, speaking both Castilian Spanish and a local version of Catalan known as Mallorquín. During the Franco regime Mallorquín was banned and you could have been imprisoned for speaking the dialect, but now it is once again recognised and can be heard throughout the island. Catalan is the official language.**

• Spaniards are the least likely European citizens to get on their bikes. They cover an average of 24km per person per year, compared with a remarkable 1,019km by the Dutch. In an attempt to encourage locals to cycle, Palma city council organises a special "Bike Day" during the St Sebastian fiestas in January and the government has opened a new stretch of "bike only" lanes in the countryside.

• **In the past, Mallorca was never famous for its olive oil. But now it has one of the best in Spain, and certainly the most expensive. It is made by the famous Dauro family, already well known for their Rioja wines. In 1996, they reintroduced the ancient *Arbequina* olive variety, first brought to the island by Jaume III in the 13th century, and in 1999 produced their first release – worth every cent.**

• Mallorcans are football crazy, with over 200 clubs in the Balearics alone. The island's leading team – Real Mallorca – has been in and out of Spanish Division One since the 1970s and reached the European Cup Winners Cup Final in 1999.

• **The Serra de Tramuntana mountains are the home of the ferreret, a small toad found nowhere else in the world. The males, which carry the eggs down to pools of water so that the eggs can develop into tadpoles, remain celibate for a month while they raise their young.**

• The island has been the subject of many novels and travelogues including *The Doll's Room* (by local writer Llorenç Villalonga) portraying life in 19th-century Mallorca; George Sand's highly critical recollections of *A Winter in Majorca*; *Jogging Round Majorca* (by Gordon West); *Problem at Pollensa Day*, a romantic short story set in pre-war Mallorca by Agatha Christie, and *Our Man in Majorca* by Tom Crichton – a witty, disaster-filled account of life as a holiday rep in the early 1960s.

Opposite: Cala Sant Viçenc, on the northern coast is a favourite Mallorcan beach

Finding Your Feet

First Two Hours

Son Sant Joan (code PMI) Airport, about 10km from Palma
city centre, serves the whole island. Some of the aeroplane
parking gates are a long way from the baggage claim area,
although there are several moving walkways. You can drive
from the airport to almost anywhere on the island within
an hour, unless you get caught in one of the summer
traffic jams.

Ground Transport Fees (excluding tip)
€ = under 5 Euros   €€ = 5–10 Euros
€€€ = 10–20 Euros   €€€€ = over 20 Euros

Airport Transfers

The **Tourism Information Centre**, just outside the baggage claim area,
provides information and advice on accommodation, attractions and trans-
portation, as well as free maps of the island. Other facilities in the arrivals
hall include currency exchange and a café.

- **Car Hire** Several international and local companies have car hire offices at
  the airport. If you don't have a hire car included in your holiday package, it
  is best to book one before you travel, especially between June and
  September. Prices are competitive, but make sure that the price includes
  unlimited mileage as well as full insurance. You will usually be expected to
  pay a credit card deposit to cover petrol and any uninsured damage that
  you cause.

- **Taxis** are available 24 hours a day and are the easiest but most expensive
  way to travel anywhere on the island. A list of prices to Palma and the
  various towns and resorts is displayed in the arrivals hall.

- **Buses** Bus No 1 runs at regular intervals from the airport into Palma, stop-
  ping at Plaça d'Espanya for the city centre and continuing to the port. From
  Plaça d'Espanya you can pick up bus and train services to other parts of
  the island.

Tourist Offices

The most helpful office in Palma is at Plaça de la Reina 2 (tel: 971 712216),
near the foot of Passeig des Born. It is open throughout the year from Monday
to Friday 9–8, Saturday 10–2. Most staff speak Spanish, English and German.
There are also tourist offices in Palma at Carrer Sant Domingo 11 and beside
the railway station in Parc de les Estacions. Most towns and seaside resorts
across the island have their own tourist offices, though some are only open
in summer.

Security

Mallorca is no more dangerous than other areas of Spain, but remember that
you are most vulnerable to theft when you arrive in an unfamiliar destination.
- Keep your hand luggage, including cameras, with you at all times.
- Do not leave any bags unattended while standing at a car hire desk or
  loading suitcases onto a bus.

Getting Around

Bus
The bus system in Mallorca is excellent and inexpensive, however it does take time to understand their timetables and to adapt your interests to their hours of operation. Ask for timetables at any tourist office or bus station.

Driving
- **Hire cars** are the most popular way to get around the island, although heavy mid-summer traffic congestion can be off-putting. Many country roads are narrow and winding.
- Carry your **driving licence** and your passport or identity card at all times. A photocopy of your passport or identity card stamped at a police station is fine, too.
- **Insurance** is recommended.
- **Parking** is often at a premium in urban areas from June to September. In cities and towns, make sure your car is properly parked in a metered area or in a car-park. In Palma, you can park in any authorised space within a blue line for up to 1.5 hours. Parking is free during siesta hours from 1:30–5 pm. Buy a ticket from the ticket machine and display it on your windscreen.
- **Seatbelts** are compulsory in Mallorca. There is a hefty fine for not wearing them.
- You may be fined on the spot for any traffic offence.
- **Speed limits** are 120kph on motorways, 90kph on other roads and 40–50kph on urban streets. Some traffic lights only turn green when you slow down to within the speed limit.

Taxis
Taxis are useful if you have not hired a car. Drivers are generally courteous and usually know the island well.

Trains
There are two railway lines in Mallorca. The main line connects Palma to Inca and Sa Pobla, with stops at Santa Maria del Camí, Binissalem and Muro. There are also five trains a day on the mountain railway from Palma to Sóller, with an optional connection to Port de Sóller by tram (► 93). The Inca and Sóller railway stations are both found on Plaça d'Espanya in Palma.

Bicycles
Cycling is the best way to travel short distances during the busy summertime, and it's a wonderful way to get around in other seasons as well.
- Most resort areas have shops where you can hire bikes at reasonable rates by the week, day or hour.
- Many town halls and tourist offices have maps suggesting routes to try out.

Walking
More and more visitors are walking longer distances. Since the island's climate is usually comfortable, you may prefer to walk. Most areas are safe for walking day and night but take the same precautions you would take at home. Maps for walking are available from good bookshops in major centres and often from tourist offices and town halls.

Accommodation

Mallorca has some 8 million visitors a year, including large numbers of British, German and Spanish tourists, and it has a wide range of accommodation to match. There are more hotel rooms in the municipality of Calvià, west of Palma, than in all of Tunisia. There are luxury resorts, palace hotels, manor house hotels, cheap hotels, apartment hotels, apartments, inns, bed and breakfasts, country farms that take in paying guests, and there are even a couple of campsites. It is best to book ahead, especially from May to October, at Easter, at Christmas and New Year, and during the late spring school holiday – the busiest seasons.

Booking Accommodation

It's usually cheaper to buy a **holiday package** with airfare and hotel included. However, if you choose to travel independently in high season, book a place to stay before you leave home. The best value-for-money places are often reserved years in advance. Accommodation prices are highest in July and August and lowest in November, December (except for Christmas and New Year), January and February: a week in summer may cost the same as a month in winter. Self-catering **aparthotels**, where maids come in to clean and change the sheets a couple of times a week, are the best value for money. Accommodation suggestions are given in later sections of this guide.

For more information, contact:
- Agroturismo (rural tourism, farmhouses and town house hotels); tel: 971 721508; fax: 971 717317; email: agroturismo@mallorcanet.com; website: www.agroturismo-balear.com.
- Reis de Mallorca (character hotels); tel: 971 770737; fax: 971 464013; email: info@reisdemallorca.com; website: www.reisdemallorca.com.

Types of Accommodation Available

Luxury resorts provide everything you need for a memorable holiday, from restaurants and swimming-pools to news-stands and entertainment every evening.

Palace hotels are former palaces that have been converted into hotels; although history buffs love them, there are some drawbacks such as windows so high up that you can't see out and many don't have lifts.

Dozens of Mallorcan **manor houses** (*fincas* or *possessiós*) have also been modernised into luxury hotels, most with swimming-pools, as well as all the beautiful blossoms and bugs of the countryside.

Some manor houses are still working farms and let out **farmstay** accommodation. Facilities vary: some have swimming-pools and others are near enough to the beach for easy access to the water.

Apartment hotels are becoming increasingly popular. Each unit has a small kitchen and most have a central reception area with bar, lounge, restaurant, swimming-pool and often a small playground for children.

The minimum stay in an **apartment** is usually a week. You can expect a fully equipped kitchen and maid service several times a week.

Inexpensive hotels or *hostales* can be comfortable but don't expect luxury.

Country villas are rented out in the same way but have the luxury of a garden.

Bed and breakfast accommodation is widely available: they offer clean and comfortable rooms, but few other services.
Various **monasteries** (➤ 14) provide inexpensive spartan overnight accommodation, usually with great views of the surrounding countryside.
Retreats and **spas**, promising to promote all-round well-being, are becoming increasingly popular with urbanites. Can Gauri (€€, Cami de Ternelles, Pollença, tel: 971 530207; email: cangauri@jet.es) is a charming old greystone millhouse; try the flotation chamber or just relax in the luscious garden.

Food and Drink

Prices
Key to prices
The € amounts in the text indicate what you can expect to pay for an average complete meal for one person, excluding drinks, tax and service charges.

€ = under €15   €€ = €15–€30   €€€ = over €30

Mallorcan gastronomy is a reflection of the surrounding sea, sunshine and rain, grazing lands and soil – and the ingenuity of its people past and present. The island has been called the breadbasket of Spain, because some of its fertile plains, when well managed, can produce three crops a year.

The original prehistoric inhabitants of the island lived peacefully, enjoying local crops and game. The Romans brought olives and wine, the Moors terraced the hillsides and planted beans, the British have brought fish and chips, and the Germans have brought *bratwurst*, *sauerkraut* and rye bread. There are Chinese, French, Indian, Irish, Italian, Moroccan, Swiss, Thai and other restaurants – the same variety of international foods found in most cosmopolitan capitals. There are also several Galician restaurants, favoured by the Spanish who know that the Gallegan kitchen is often superior to any other in Spain.

Mallorcan Cuisine
- Local dishes, based on plants and animals that flourish on the island, are often the best. What the chef finds in the market in the morning largely determines the highlights of the midday and evening meals in his or her restaurant. If you want to eat well, ask about the special of the day. Mallorcan cuisine is merely a variation of Catalan cuisine, famous the world over for variety and flavour. It's often hard to choose between the sweet, flavourful fruit and deliciously tempting pastry as dessert.
- Nearly every meal starts with bread and olives (often the tart green olives typical of the island), although butter is usually available upon request. There are fresh salads in summer while hearty broths brighten damp winter days.
- There are vegetable *cocas* (a first cousin to pizza), rice dishes and vegetable stews. Although beef has never been a local speciality, the fish, seafood, pork, lamb, rabbit, kid, chicken and eggs can be excellent, and most are cooked with olive oil, renowned as a healthy alternative to other oils and fats. Almond cake, flan and ice-cream are popular desserts.
- Island wines are excellent and so is Spanish beer. Local drinks include *palo*, a thick brown aperitif made from carob beans, along with *hierbas* a dry or sweet liqueur made from local herbs including fennel and anise, believed to help digestion and promote good health. Fresh orange juice, lemonade and *horchata de chufa* (almond milk) are other tasty specialities.

Good Deal

Restaurants vary from ultra-expensive to cheap. Like all Spaniards, Mallorcans eat their biggest meal in the middle of the day, rarely starting before 1:30, although most restaurants open at noon for visitors. The best deal is often the *menú del día* (menu of the day), posted in front of the restaurant. This three-course meal with wine or water, especially in inland villages and at motorway service areas, can cost less than a cappuccino at an elegant Northern European hotel. Mallorcans tend to eat very late, especially in summer, with dinner usually taken at around 9 or 10 pm.

If you want to eat in a hurry, the best bet is a bar serving *tapas* (➤ 17).

Reserving a Table

Many restaurants do not take reservations, but in summer, it's advisable to book a table for dinner if you're planning to eat at a popular or expensive restaurant.

Recommended Places to Eat and Drink

Each of the five sections in this book, covering different areas of the island, lists recommended places to eat and drink. These are listed alphabetically and price guidelines are indicated. Restaurants frequently change ownership and management, so it's a good idea to confirm current quality in food and service.

Taxes and service charges are often automatically included in the price. Spaniards rarely tip, except for any loose small change floating around in their pockets. Waiters have come to expect foreigners to tip up to 10 per cent for good meal service.

Wine

The winegrowing tradition in the Balearics dates back to the time of Roman rule. The prestigious wines made from grapes cultivated in the Binissalem area carry a guarantee of origin and quality. Also renowned are several varieties of local wines from the Petra region.

The red house wine in most restaurants is very drinkable, although sometimes the white house wine is a little sweet.

Bests...

... **almond ice-cream:** Can Joan de s'Aigo, Palma (➤ 60)
... **café/bar scene:** Bar Els Casinet, Port de Pollença (➤ 129)
... **café for people-watching:** Wellies, Puerto Portals (➤ 81)
... **coffee and ensaimadas:** Can Joan de s'Aigo, Palma (➤ 60)
... **cybercafé:** L@ Red Cybercafé, Palma (➤ 62)
... **hotel restaurant:** Es Reco de Randa, Randa (➤ 150)
... **suckling pig:** Celler Can Amer, Inca (➤ 151)
... **menú del día (lunch only):** Mesón Son Caliu, Palma Nova (➤ 79)
... **monastery meal:** Lluc (➤ 104)
... **paella:** Parlament, Palma (➤ 62)
... **pizza:** Vecchio Giovanni, Palma (➤ 63)
... **salad:** La Taberna del Caracol, Palma (➤ 62)
... **seafood:** Koldo Royo, Palma (➤ 61)
... **stuffed aubergines:** L'Aup, Cala Sant Vicenç road (➤ 130)
... **restaurant with a view:** Mirador Ses Barques, Sóller (➤ 105)

Shopping

Every day is outdoor market day somewhere on the island; check with your hotel to find one near by.

The outdoor markets (see Sineu Market, ► 144) are fun, the prices, sometimes negotiable, are as good as anywhere and the variety of goods extensive. There is fresh produce, marinated olives, sausages and cheeses. There are clothes, shoes and other leather products like purses and belts. Craft stalls, manned by numerous nationalities from Africa and Europe, sell jewellery, candles, handmade paper, wood carvings and an assortment of other goods. Browsing is a popular pastime accepted by both market vendors and shopkeepers. But they do not like you to touch and rearrange too much. The best department store is El Corte Inglés (► 63): there is a good variety of goods, staff are well trained and prices are reasonable.

Clothing

Palma has the widest variety of shops, although you can find bargains and quality items in most towns. Leather-trimmed sweater jackets for men, so practical for damp winters, are a wonderful bargain as are leather bags, belts and shoes. Designer shops, both on the main streets and tucked away in unlikely corners in the old part of Palma, are fun to explore. Department stores offer a vast range of clothes, both Spanish and imported at good prices. Some supermarkets sell inexpensive clothes and small appliances, in case you forget to bring something vital with you.

Jewellery

The best place to buy Mallorcan handmade pearls is El Corte Inglés, although they are also sold at souvenir shops all over the island and at factory shops in Manacor. High-quality jewellery shops dot the streets in downtown Palma. Outdoor market stalls sell jewellery for every occasion and season.

Leather

Spain is justly famous for quality leather and suede at reasonable prices. Although most leather factories and outlets are located in Inca (► 153), every resort, town and nearly every village sells footwear, jackets, belts, wallets and so on, in an assortment of qualities, designs and prices.

Art

Mallorcan art is for sale at every turn. Mallorca has encouraged artists for generations and Mallorcans have been hanging original paintings on their walls for centuries. Many hotels, restaurants, cafés and bars, large and small, are plastered with paintings, varying from local landscapes to modern abstracts. Should you see one you like, ask the management about it. Almost everything is for sale if the price is right.

Crafts

■ With so many beautiful **ceramic** and **pottery** pieces around, the only problem is deciding what to buy and whether you can manage to carry it home. Perhaps the most typical Mallorcan craft, but the most difficult to bring home without breakage, is the *siurell*, a clay figurine painted white and trimmed with short bold strokes of red and green. Each *siurell* has a small whistle, which sounds vaguely like a flute, cut into it. Many come from the Marratxi, a Palma suburb, known as the land of clay.

- **Olive wood** is hardy enough to last several lifetimes. For bowls, carvings, jewellery and trinkets, visit the factory outlet in Manacor (➤ 153). Most weekly markets also sell some olive-wood items.

- **Tablecloths, place mats** and **napkins** with embroidered flowers, often in blue, are a Mallorcan tradition. Beautiful as they are, most need heavy ironing. A traditional island fabric pattern, known as *roba de llengues* (tongues), also needs ironing but will last a lifetime and will serve to bring back memories of Mallorca for years to come. Some are woven and some are printed; the pattern is vaguely reminiscent of the waves of the sea or the furrows in a farm field. You'll find an excellent selection at Galeries Vicenç on the north side of the roundabout just east of Pollença.

- **Foodstuffs** are probably the most popular souvenir – a great way to share your holiday with family, friends and neighbours. At Palma airport you will see departing visitors carrying stacks of round card-board boxes colourfully decorated with Mallorcan motifs. Inside are *ensaimadas*, the light breakfast pastries that melt in the mouth. You can order them at a bakery the day before you are scheduled to leave or pick them up at a shop in the airport.

Prices

Prices of goods are quoted in Euros (➤ 171) and are generally not nego-tiable, although there's little to lose by suggesting a discount, especially if you are buying in quantity. If you're shopping seriously, with extra time and energy, look in several shops, since prices frequently vary greatly from one shop to the next. Credit cards are accepted in department stores and major shops, but not by market traders. Small shops sometimes are reluctant to accept credit cards, even though they may be advertised in the window.

Opening Times

- Markets are usually open from 8 am to 1 pm, although trading times vary with the season, the number of shoppers around and other events of the day.

- Shop opening hours are usually Monday to Friday from 9:30 am to 1:30 pm and from 4:30 pm to 7:30 or 8 pm. Some shops stay open later in summer to entice after-dinner strollers. On Saturday and Sunday, most shops are often open only in the morning. Some big shopping centres and supermarkets do not close for siesta.

Bests...
...**antiques:** Del Monte, La Rambla 8, Palma, tel: 971 715047
...**art bookshop:** Llibreria des Call, Carrer Call 8, Palma
...**bread:** Can Banya, Carrer Sant Domingo 11, Pollença
...**Mallorcan crafts:** Galeries Vicenç, Pollença (➤ 131)
...**cosmetics:** Selecta, Oms 5, Palma
...**department store:** El Corte Inglés (➤ 63)
...**designer clothes:** The Best, Passeig Anglada Camarasa 7, Port de Pollença
...**electronics:** Continente, Cardenal Rossell s/n, Palma
...**flea market:** Consell (Sunday mornings) (➤ 153)
...**old neighbourhood to explore:** around Palma's cathedral (➤ 46)
...**teenage accessories:** El Corte Inglés, Palma (➤ 63)
...**toy shop:** Imaginarium, Plaça Weyler s/n, Palma

Entertainment

Your hotel receptionists, **The Reader** (a weekly) and the **Majorca Daily Bulletin** English-language newspapers (available at most news kiosks), and the **Events** sheet published quarterly by the tourist office are all good sources of information about what's on. Entertainment varies from a splashy Las Vegas-style dinner show at the Casino west of Palma to people-watching at a pavement café.

Theatre, Music and Disco

Palma attracts world-class entertainers year round, as does the auditorium and several night-clubs in Alcúdia. Numerous entrepreneurs have dedicated energy and expertise to developing entertainment that appeals to both residents and visitors. The Conselleria de Turisme sponsors "A Winter In Mallorca", a series of free concerts from November to April. Most are held in beautiful old churches and cloisters around the island.

Fiestas

There's a fiesta every month somewhere on the island. Ask about local fiestas as soon as you arrive. That way, you will be able to join the celebrations if you want to, and you will know when the banks and post office will be closed.

Fiestas

5 January	**Parade of the Three Kings** at Palma and Port de Pollença
17 January	**Sant Antoni Blessing of the Animals** at Palma, Sa Pobla and Artá
February	**Sa Rua Carnival** – a grand parade through Palma and fancy dress parades and parties in almost every town on the island
March/April	**Easter processions** at Palma, Sineu and Pollença
May	**Mock battle** between Moors and Christians at Sóller on second Sunday of the month
13 June	**Corpus Christi Dance of the Eagles** – local girls dress like eagles at Pollença
16 July	**Verge del Carme Day** – the blessing of the fleet at Port d'Andratx, Cala Ratjada, Port de Pollença and Port de Sóller
2 August	**Mock battle** between Moors and Christians at Pollença
24 August	**Sant Bartomeu Fiesta** with horse races at Capdepera
September	**Autumn wine festival** at Binissalem on last Sunday of the month
October	**"La Beateta"** parade around Palma honouring Santa Catalina Thomàs on third Saturday of the month
Mid-November	**Dijous Bo** fair – the largest commercial fair with market, animals and playground at Inca
31 December	**Festa de l'Estendard** – Palma celebrates the Christian conquest by Jaume I in 1229

Outdoor Action

- The Conselleria de Turisme publishes a series of brochures on such themes as beaches, cycling, cruising, golf, active tourism, recreation areas and nature reserves. Walkers may wish to consult *Classic Hikes Through Mallorca* by Herbert Heinrich.
- The Mediterranean is the setting for swimming, pedaloing, water-skiing, snorkelling, scuba-diving, sailing, parasailing, windsurfing and canoeing or kayaking. The sky overhead offers opportunities for gliding, ultralight flying, parapenting and helicopter sightseeing tours. The land invites ramblers, rock-climbers, cyclists, golfers, horse-riders and pot-holers.
- Organised action-packed holidays vary from week-long courses in scuba-diving and sailing to escorted hikes of hill and vale every day of the week. It's best to book this kind of holiday in advance to ensure you get what you want.

Bookings

Any hotel desk or tourist office can point you in the right direction, and possibly provide maps, information on organised events and even make bookings. For further information about what's on, these websites are worth visiting:
www.visitbalearis.com
www.majorcadailybulletin.es

Admission Charges

The cost of admission for museums and other places of interest mentioned in the text is indicated by three price categories:
Inexpensive under €3   **Moderate** €3–€6   **Expensive** over €6

TOURIST OFFICES IN MALLORCA

Most tourism offices are open Monday to Saturday mornings in summer and some of the major offices are also open on weekday afternoons; times vary the rest of the year. Check with the tourist office at Palma airport first.

Son Sant Joan Airport
Tel/fax: 971 789556

Palma
Plaça de la Reina, 2
Tel: 971 712216
Fax: 971 720251

Magaluf
Avinguda Pere Vaquer Ramis 1
Tel: 971 131126
Fax: 971 131188

Palma Nova
Passeig de la Mar 13
Tel/fax: 971 682365

Pollença
Carrer Guillem Cifre
Tel: 971 535077

Port d'Alcúdia
Carretera d'Artà 68
Tel/fax: 971 892615

Port de Pollença
Carrer de les Monges 9
Tel: 971 865467
Fax: 971 866746

Sóller
Plaça d'Espanya
Tel: 971 638008

Palma

Getting Your Bearings

Gothic, modernist, affluent and chic, the capital of the
Balearic islands is one of Europe's most exciting and
appealing cities. The setting alone is magnificent,
gently curving around a broad, sheltered bay.
Half of Mallorca's population live here and to
many islanders it is known simply as *Ciutat*
(City). This is where you will find the
best restaurants and shops, together
with a host of historic sights. Palma is
easily reached by bus or car from
anywhere on Mallorca and you are
really missing out if you do
not spend a day soaking
up the atmosphere
of its streets
and squares.

PICASSO

SON'
ESPANYOLE

AVINGUDA

SON
COTONE

Poble
Espanyol **12**

SON
DURETA

ANDREA

DORIA

CARRETERA AL
CASTELL DE BELLVER

The narrow
streets of Old
Palma shade
strollers from
the sun

*Parc
Bellver*

II Castell
de Bellver

PASSEIG MARÍTIM

10
Harbourf
and port

AVINGUDA DE JOAN MIRÓ

EL TERRENO

AV GABRIEL ROCA

Club de Mar

The classic image of Palma is the view from
the waterfront, best appreciated on a boat
trip around the bay. As you approach the
harbour, the cathedral and royal palace seem
to rise out of the city walls, their golden
sandstone lit up by the afternoon sun and
reflected in an artificial lake. Behind them is
the old Arab quarter, a warren of medieval
lanes where the Catalan merchants built
their palaces, their elegant courtyards and
patios survive today. The huge wooden doors
along Carrer Morey are open to the street,

★ Don't Miss

At Your Leisure

Badia de Palma

Page 41: La Seu and Palau de l'Almudaina dominate the city of Palma

offering a glimpse of these courtyards with their stone steps, arcaded balconies and urns overflowing with potted plants.

Modern Palma is a city of the streets, bursting with creativity and buzzing with life. Stroll along the tree-lined boulevards of La Rambla and Passeïg des Born, admiring the flower stalls and the passing parade of humanity; explore the craft shops and art galleries in the streets around Plaça Major; sip coffee at dusk in the designer bars and cafés along the seafront promenade, or take cocktails in a 17th-century palace, and you will understand why Palma has been voted the city with the best quality of life in Spain (➤ 30).

Spend the morning exploring Palma's history and the afternoon relaxing on the waterfront as you soak up the atmosphere of Mallorca's capital.

Palma in a Day

10:00 am

Begin in Parc de la Mar (➤ 55), gazing up at the cathedral through a forest of palm trees as you stand on land reclaimed from the sea. Climb the stairs to the medieval walls and plunge into the old Arab quarter, admiring the courtyards along Carrer Morey before visiting the Banys Àrabs (pictured left, ➤ 55).

11:30 am

Return to the walls and climb the steps to visit La Seu (➤ 46), then take a tour of Palau de l'Almudaina (➤ 49). Afterwards, you can relax in the old royal gardens, Hort del Rei, with their fountains, orange trees and modern sculptures.

1:00 pm

Select a table in the sun outside Taberna la Bóveda (➤ 62) and choose from a wide selection of *tapas* accompanied by a plate of *pa amb oli*.

2:30 pm

Work off your lunch with a stroll along the seafront (➤ 51), passing the fishing port and continuing around the harbour with Castell de Bellver visible in the distance. When you reach the pleasure-boat jetty, turn around and walk back – the views the other way, of the cathedral across the bay, are even more stunning.

4:00 pm

Treat yourself to tea and cakes at El Pesquero, a fishermen's bar turned into a chic boardwalk café with a terrace overlooking the port. Then take a taxi to Castell de Bellver (courtyard pictured above, ➤ 53) to admire the *bell ver* (beautiful view) of Palma Bay from the roof-top.

6:00 pm

Walk down through the pine woods and hop on a bus to return to central Palma. This is the time to take part in the *paseo*, a stroll along La Rambla (➤ 57) combined with an early-evening drink and a spot of window-shopping in the streets around Plaça Major (right, ➤ 57).

8:30 pm

Make your way back down to the waterfront for dinner at one of the fish restaurants on the quay. After dinner, head for cocktails at Abaco, Palma's classiest bar. If that doesn't sound like your scene, join a younger, trendier set at Varadero, a terrace bar at the end of the quay with fabulous views of the cathedral (detail from cathedral door pictured left). Remember, in Palma, the night is still young...

La Seu

La Seu (Palma Cathedral) is the symbol of Palma and a masterpiece of Catalan Gothic architecture, one of the finest Gothic churches in all of Spain and certainly the most spectacularly sited.

This is a building designed to be admired from the sea, a striking symbol of Christian might to deter any potential invaders. Start your exploration on the south front, overlooking the harbour, where flying buttresses loom large over the sandstone walls. The south front also contains the most impressive external feature, the Portal del Mirador, a Gothic doorway dating from the late-14th century. The door jambs feature exquisitely sculpted statues of St James, St John the Baptist, St Peter, St Paul and St Andrew, while the mullion dividing the doorway supports a sculpture of the Mirador

Detail from a relief depicting the Assumption of the Virgin on the west door of La Seu

✚ 177 D2 ✉ Palau Reial 29
☎ 971 723130 🕑 Mon–Fri 10–6, Sat 10–2, Apr–Oct; Mon–Fri 10–2:30, Sat 10–1:30, rest of year; closed Sun
♿ Inexpensive

Virgin. Above the doorway, the tympanum shows God the Father and six adoring angels hovering over a splendid relief of the Last Supper.

From here you can walk around to the main west front, completed in 1601 but later destroyed by an earthquake and rebuilt in neo-Gothic style in the late-19th century. The actual entrance to the cathedral is further round, through the Portal del Almoina, situated on the north front beneath the bell tower.

Unless you are coming for a service, you enter through the cathedral museum, where various treasures and religious artefacts are displayed in the chapter house and sacristy. If you are short of time, skip this and head straight for the nave; the best place to take it all in is from the great west door. The vast interior, with its 87 windows, is a monument to light and

The evening skyline of Palma's harbour is dominated by the illuminated cathedral

Detail from the rose window, 30 metres above the floor

shadow. The great rose window over the presbytery is one of the biggest and best from Gothic times. It stretches 12m across, with a surface area of 100sq m, and is divided into 24 triangles, half of which form the Star of David. It has been rebuilt several times since it was first created some seven centuries ago.

The central nave is flanked by aisles with eight side chapels each. The slender pillars which divide the nave from the aisles are ringed with wrought-iron candelabra by Antoni Gaudí. It was Gaudí who was instrumental in moving the choir loft from the centre of the cathedral to the Capella Reial (Royal Chapel) behind the high altar. Gaudí also created the porcelain plant motifs and the coats of arms of bishops which surround the 13th-century Bishop's Throne, and the Crown of Thorns canopy over the altar (➤ 24). Behind the Royal Chapel, the Trinity Chapel contains the tombs of the Mallorcan kings Jaume II and Jaume III.

TAKING A BREAK

Two blocks west of the cathedral, across Es Born, Taberna La Bóveda (➤ 62) provides great respite from serious sight-seeing. You can have a simple coffee or beer or a full meal at the sunny outdoor tables.

LA SEU: INSIDE INFO

Top tip Be sure to visit the cathedral on a sunny day, for its spectacular **stained-glass windows** are at their best in bright sunshine.

• Kids will probably love the **macabre** skull and crossbones, with the hourglass, inset into the floor at the centre front of the cathedral. The brass cherub playing the flute, also a part of the floor, is happy by contrast.

• You can get into the cathedral for **free** by going to High Mass, held on Sundays at 10:30.

Palau de l'Almudaina

Islamic and Gothic architecture are harmoniously combined in this splendid royal palace, a centre of power in Mallorca for more than 2,000 years. The Romans built a settlement here and the Arabs made it their fortress, parts of which have been incorporated into the Catalan Gothic design.

🕂 176 C2 ✉ Carrer del Palau Reial
☎ 971 714368
🕐 Mon–Fri 10–6 (closed 2–4 Oct–Mar);
Sat and holidays 10–2; closed Sun
💶 Inexpensive

The original Moorish beauty of the Palau de l'Almudaina was rejuvenated by restoration in 1918

One of the
many striking
tapestries
housed in
Palau de
l'Almudaina

The Catalans, after conquering Mallorca from the Moors in 1229, rebuilt the palace for their Mallorcan kings and governors, and the Almudaina remains an official royal residence today for the King and Queen of Spain to entertain special visitors. The building also contains a museum and is the military headquarters for the Balearic Islands.

The southern façade is truly magnificent, seen from the Passeig Marítim and the harbour. The first floor features four rounded arches, the second floor has eight pointed arches, while the third and top floor has four double-arched windows. Look out for the Angel Tower, crowned by a statue of the archangel Gabriel dating from 1309. Inside, the main entrance (opposite the cathedral) leads to the King's Patio which dates from the 14th century and houses the royal chapel of Santa Ana. The smaller Queen's Patio, with a porticoed gallery and twin windows, features the St James Chapel. Perhaps the most impressive room in the palace is the Tinell or throne room, where pointed arches spring directly from the floor to support a main beam and a wooden roof with two slopes.

TAKING A BREAK
About a block north is the Parlament (➤ 62), a great spot for a sip of sherry or tea at the bar or for a paella lunch.

Palau de l'Almudaina
Located in the Hort del Rei Gardens, the Moorish Drassana Arch spans 18m to support the narrow bridge which once led to the inner harbour. Moorish-Mallorcan emirs residing in the Almudaina Palace enjoyed private moorage at their doorstep and direct access to the sea. Hidden for centuries, the slightly elliptical arch was discovered and restored during renovation work on the Almudaina in 1961.

Harbourfront and Port

The Palma seafront, with its beautiful rounded bay, has been a welcome platform for visitors since tourism began on the island, and the harbour became busier than ever when the city was settled as a port. It's a wonderful walk from Parc de la Mar along the seafront to the passenger ship terminal at the west end of the harbour. A 5-km long paved path for cyclists, skateboarders, rollerbladers and joggers now borders the sea side of this broad boulevard, which was built in the 1950s to link the old port of Palma, Porto Pi, with the city centre. Shops, cafés and restaurants line the promenade. If you prefer a fast track, take a taxi or horse and carriage there or back.

Palma's commercial and leisure docks show the city at its prettiest

Just west of the statue of Ramón Llull, at the roundabout near the Palau de l'Almudaina, the Passeìg de Sagrera, shaded by tall graceful palms, is bordered by the 15th-century La Llotja, designed by Mallorcan architect Guillem Sagrera as a place for merchants and

✚ 179 D2
Mare Nostrum Excursions
✉ Passeig Marítim 33 ☎ 971 456182; www.marenostrum-catamarans.com 🕐 May–Oct, cruises at 10 and 3:30 💲 Expensive

businessmen to trade, but now a provincial museum which houses temporary exhibitions. The 17th-century galleried Consulat del Mar now houses a maritime museum and government offices. At the west end of the Passeìg stands a statue of Nicaraguan poet Rubén Dario who made his home in La Cartoixa, Valldemossa (➤ 88), and wrote poetry about the monastery and village. The Passeig de Sagrera continues as the Passeìg Marítim (Paseo Marítimo).

Although the fishing port is no longer as active as it once was, because Mediterranean sealife has been diminishing, fishermen still sit in the sun and mend their nets. If you look east from this dock behind their boats, you'll have a splendid view of the cathedral. Near by is an intriguing two-sided sundial.

On the next dock west, beyond a monument to medieval

For centuries, Mallorcan fishermen have been captivated by the allure of the sea

cartographers, a fleet of pleasure craft offers excursions around the harbour – morning, afternoon, all day or possibly a catamaran champagne sunset cruise. You can sail away for a memorable day with a barbecue buffet lunch with Mare Nostrum Excursions aboard their catamaran, the *Magic*. The afternoon sail provides drinks and snacks, and there is a champagne cruise at sunset.

The Club de Mar Marina harbours luxurious yachts, while the Estació Marítimo, with its international cruise ships, naval vessels and ferries to other Balearic Islands and the Spanish mainland, anchors the western end of the waterfront.

TAKING A BREAK

El Pesquero, overlooking the fishing port, is a good place for a drink or a snack on the boardwalk terrace in summer.

HARBOURFRONT AND PORT: INSIDE INFO

Top tip The harbourfront walk is particularly attractive during the evening, as the sun sets over the harbour and the cathedral lights up for the night.

Hidden gem Just beyond the fishing port, look out for the oratory of Sant Elm, a sailors' chapel moved here stone by stone in 1947 and set in its own small garden.

Castell de Bellver

The name of this castle means "lovely view" in Catalan and it is easy to understand why as you stand on the roof-top balcony looking down over the city and Palma Bay.

The castle, the only circular one in Spain, is supported by three semicircular buttressed towers, while a fourth tower rises 7m from the body of the castle. The two-storey structure is constructed around a circular courtyard. The main floor features exquisite rounded arches that play so well with light

For the best view of Castell de Bellver, head out to the hills behind Cala Major

✚ 179 D2
✉ Parc Bellver, El Terreno ☎ 971 730657
🕑 Mon–Sat 8 am–8:30 pm, Sun 10–7, Apr–Sep; Mon–Sat 8–7:15, Sun 10–5, rest of year
🚌 3, 4, 20, 21, 22 to Plaça Gomila 💷 Inexpensive

and shade, while the second floor sports pointed Gothic arches and ribbed vaults.

The fortress is so well preserved that it's hard to believe it was built 700 years ago during the reign of Jaume II. In 1717, the castle became a military prison. In the early 1800s Treasury Minister Gaspar Melchor was imprisoned here during the reign of Carlos IV, as later were French officers and soldiers who had been defeated in the Battle of Bailen. General Lacy, leader of a failed rebellion, faced a firing squad here in 1817. The castle was used as a mint in 1821.

The Balearic government gave the castle to the City of Palma in 1931, who turned it into a public park and local history museum. The top floor shelters the Despuig Collection, one of the best

Pere Salvà, who built Castell de Bellver, also remodelled the Almudaina Palace

small collections of classical sculptures you'll find anywhere, including a fine statue of a nude male, an intriguing Medusa and an exquisite white marble sculpture of a beautiful young woman peacefully sleeping on her bed.

TAKING A BREAK

The Porto Pi Shopping Centre is just a few blocks away on the waterfront. Try Frommos cheese delicatessen, where you can sip a glass of wine and sample dozens of different cheeses.

CASTELL DE BELLVER: INSIDE INFO

Top tip Be sure to look down inside the square well in the middle of the circular courtyard to see the wonderful ivy and fern garden which has grown around the walls.

• Buses to Castell de Bellver stop at Plaça Gomila, from where it is a steep climb to the castle through the pine woods. Take a taxi instead and save your energy for the walk down, then return to Palma by bus or along the seafront promenade.

One to miss If you're short of time, don't bother with the city history museum, which mostly contains dull fragments from archaeological digs.

In more depth If you've enjoyed the Despuig Collection of sculptures, you might like to visit Cardinal Despuig's 18th-century estate at Raixa, where Italianate gardens are open to the public. The estate is signposted on the Palma–Sóller road just south of Bunyola (Wed–Sun 11–5, in winter, 11–7, in summer).

At Your Leisure

1 Parc de la Mar

Just south of La Seu and the old city wall is a peaceful park of palm-shaded terraces, walkways and cafés where Palmesanos retreat from office overload. Parc de la Mar was created in the 1960s on land reclaimed from the sea following the building of the Passeig Marítim. To some it is an example of concrete brutality, to others it is one of the most beautiful spots in Palma. The centrepiece is an artificial lake, created to reflect the cathedral in the way that Palma Bay used to. Beside the lake is a large, colourful mural by the Catalan artist Joan Miró, a gift to his adopted city. Between the inside and outside city walls, in the filled-in moat, is Ses Voltes, a space set aside for outdoor concerts and exhibitions. Cafés within the park serve drinks and snacks, and there is also a playground for children.

➕ 177 D1

2 Banys Àrabs

The Banys Àrabs (Arab Baths) are one of the few surviving monuments from the period of Moorish rule on Mallorca, which lasted from 902 to 1229 AD. Located in the classical garden of Can Fontiroig, they are thought to date from the early-12th century and were part of a palace belonging to an Arab nobleman.

The baths were built in Roman style and were used as meeting-places and pleasure centres. Signs of the chimneys can still be seen in the stonework and the remains of steam and water conduits are visible on the floor.

Bathers followed a narrow passage leading to a changing chamber, and from there, they entered the tepidarium, the smaller room with the vaulted ceiling. From the tepid waters they went to the square main room, the caldarium, for hot baths, where 12 cylindrical columns form

One of the colourful paintings which can be seen at the Museu de Mallorca

horseshoe arches, capped by a cupola containing 25 small round skylights. The capitals are not identical, probably because the Moors often recycled materials from older buildings, both Roman and Moorish.

The garden, perhaps the most evocative area of all with its cacti, palms, orange trees and fountains, is an excellent place to relax and reflect.

➕ 177 D2
✉ Carrer de Can Serra 7
☎ 971 721549
🕐 Daily 9:30–7   💶 Inexpensive

3 Museu de Mallorca

If you really want to learn about Mallorca's history visit the Museu de Mallorca, the island's most comprehensive history museum, located within the 17th-century palace, Ca la Gran Cristiana, built on the foundations of an old Moorish home. The grand patio leads to various rooms wherein artefacts and art tell the tales of different eras in Mallorcan history: the peaceful Bronze-Age Talaiots, the

colonis-
ing Romans,
the magnificent Moors
and the conquering Christians.

✠ 177 D2
✉ Carrer de la Portella 5
☎ 971 717540 🕐 Tue–Sat 9:30–1:30,
4–6, Sun 10–2, Nov–May; Tue–Wed and
Fri–Sat 10–2, 5–7, Thu 10–2, 6–9, Sun
10–2, rest of year 💶 Inexpensive

6 Basílica i Claustre de Sant Francesc

This Gothic church is well worth a
short visit inside and out – inside for
the tomb of Ramón Llull, the Stephen
Hawking of his day, and outside for
the exquisite 14th-century cloister.

It's challenging to find Llull's tomb
because the church interior is so
dark, but it is
located in a
trapezoidal chapel on
the left-hand side near the front.
Push the tiny timed light switch on
the wall to light up the alcove. The
tomb, which seems rather small, was
built of alabaster in 1487 and depicts
the prostrate figure of the illustrious
scholar and scientist. The seven
empty niches below were supposed
to have been filled with statues rep-
resenting the arts, but five centuries
later they're still empty.

The cloister, next to the church,
is an oasis of peace and has been
declared a national monument. Among

**The Franciscans built the Sant Francesc
Basilica and its courtyard on the site of an
old Moorish soap factory**

the lawns and lemon trees, walkways lead to a central fountain dating from 1638 which displays the coat of arms of Bishop Joan of Santander.

The panelled wooden roof of the surrounding four galleries features the coats of arms of Catalan–Aragón royalty. The 115 columns, joined by pointed lobular archways, give the cloister a Moorish flavour. The north gallery, the earliest, has alternating thick and thin columns, while the other galleries have uniform columns, but more ornate arches. The upper gallery, added in the 16th and 17th centuries, has octagonal columns. The walls and floors of the galleries contain the tombstones of 72 noble families.

➕ 177 E2
✉ Plaça de Sant Francesc
☎ 971 712695
🕐 Daily 9:30–12:30, 3:30–6, Sun and holidays 9:30–12:30 💶 Inexpensive

🛇 Plaça Major

This plaza was built a decade after the Inquisition headquarters on the site were demolished in the early 1800s. Four floors with long green shutters run around the perimeter, while the portico with its dozens of ground-floor arches hides a variety of shops. The plaza was the site of an important fish and vegetable market until it was closed in 1951 and

Shops line the steps leading from Plaça Weyler to Plaça Major

moved to a larger site. During excavation for the car-park underneath in the late 1960s, remains of a fortified Moorish wall were unearthed on the north side. The 13th-century scholar and missionary Ramón Llull was born in a house on this square although his home is long gone. Today, the pedestrian-only plaza is a pleasant place to pause, for there are several pavement cafés where musicians entertain and artisans sell their crafts. If you have restless children, not to worry; right outside the plaza is a Disney store.

➕ 177 E3

🛇 La Rambla (Vía Roma)

In 1613 this promenade was built on the bed of a diverted wash which in times past had resulted in disastrous floods. During the mid-1800s, the street was remodelled, plane trees were planted and the 12-sided fountain was installed at the north end. Two sculptures of handsome ancient Romans at the south end overlook an abstract trio of fallen arches and the stairway to the Plaça Major. Vía Roma is a beautiful place to stroll and admire the many flowers at various stalls.

➕ 177 D4

The Gran Hotel was the predecessor of many modern Mallorcan hotels

9 Gran Hotel (Fundació la Caixa)

This handsome five-storey art nouveau building, originally created in 1902 as the first grand hotel of Palma, was renovated and restored in 1993 by la Caixa, a popular Catalan bank. The magnificent modernist exterior is a whimsical wonder of columns, arches and balconies trimmed with colourful ceramic tiles. The stained-glass windows are also beautiful. The Gran Hotel is no longer a hotel, but a cultural centre. La Caixa Foundation creates and presents educational, cultural, social and environmental programmes via courses, lectures, concerts and exhibitions. The permanent art collection comprises 80 oil paintings and 125 drawings by Pollençan post-Impressionist artist Anglada Camarasa (1871–1959). The various temporary exhibits are usually excellent. The ground floor has a good restaurant (El Café, ➤ 61) and bar, along with a bookshop for browsing, especially for art books.

✚ 177 D3
✉ Plaça Weyler 3
☎ 971 178500; fax: 971 722120; email: ccpalma.fundacio@lacaixa.es
🕓 Tue–Sat 10–9, Sun and holidays 10–2 Free

12 Poble Espanyol (Pueblo Español)

Walled like a medieval city, this theme park contains two dozen mini-reproductions of castles, palaces, fortresses, homes and monuments from all over Spain. Here you can see scaled-down versions of such Spanish landmarks as Sevilla's Giraldo Tower, Granada's Alhambra, El Greco's home in Toledo and a Canary Islands house complete with latticed wooden balcony. There is also an intriguing animated exhibit of agricultural life past and present around Mallorca. Poble Espanyol is dotted with assorted cafés, bars and restaurants. Hands-on workshops demonstrate crafts varying from woodworking to lace-making.

✚ 179 D2 ✉ Carrer de Poble Espanyol 39 ☎ 971 737075
🕓 Daily 9–8, Apr–Nov; 9–6, rest of year 🚌 4, 5, taxi Moderate

Potters and other artisans demonstrate their crafts at Poble Espanyol

Where to... Stay

Prices

Prices are for the least expensive double room in high season, IVA sales tax included. Prices may drop by up to 50 per cent in low season. Breakfast is usually included in the room price. € = under 60 Euros €€ = 60–120 Euros €€€ = over 120 Euros

Like most regional capital cities, Palma has a good range of accommodation types from top-class international chains to inexpensive hostels for the budget conscious.

Born €€

This two-star hotel near the top of Passeig des Born is the best place to stay if you are looking for charm, character and a central location at a reasonable price. It is set behind huge wooden doors inside a 16th-century palace, with a delightful courtyard of palm trees. You can take breakfast in the courtyard in summer. Although the hotel is showing its age and is looking a little care-worn in places, the rooms are comfortable enough, and all have the benefit of air-conditioning and central heating. The elegant shops of Avinguda Jaume III are just around the corner and the seafront is only a short stroll away.

🕇 176 C3
✉ Carrer Sant Jaume 3
☎ 971 712942;
email: **hotel-born@hotmail.com**;
www.hotelborn.com

Dalt Murada €€€

This elegant Gothic mansion near the cathedral has been carefully restored and turned into a luxury hotel with just three double rooms and five suites, decorated with rugs, tapestries and 18th-century furniture. All of the rooms have mod cons such as air-conditioning, mini-bars, satellite TV and internet access, and some have their own Jacuzzi and private terrace. A good base for a romantic weekend in the heart of the old town.

🕇 177 D2 ✉ Carrer Almudaina 6A
☎ 971 425300; fax: 971 719708;
email: **info@daltmurada.com**;
www.daltmurada.com

Palacio Ca Sa Galesa €€€

This small but splendid 17th-century palace, a great B&B base for exploring Palma, sits in the heart of the old town behind the cathedral. But inside the wrought-iron gates and past the patio (where you can park your car) is another world – a soothing combination of luxurious antique furnishings, modern comforts and friendly, efficient service. All 12 rooms are named after famous pieces of music, so if you want the best room in the house, just ask for Gershwin's *Rhapsody in Blue*. The vaulted basement, containing a small swimming-pool, sauna and exercise equipment, is thought to have had Roman origins. A great bonus is the complimentary afternoon tea in the Monet kitchen or in the elegant high-ceilinged salon with its generous collection of colourful coffee-table books.

🕇 177 D2 ✉ Miramar 8 ☎ 971 715400; fax: 971 721579; email: **reservas@palaciocasagalesa.com**; **www.palaciocasagalesa.com**

Ritzi €

This simple *hostal*, just off Es Born in the heart of the scenic old town, provides basic rooms for budget-minded travellers. All rooms have basins with hot water but some only have shared bath or shower facilities – check when booking your accommodation. Plaça La Llotja, where *la movida* throbs as the stars come out, is only a short distance away.

➕ 176 B3 ✉ Apuntadores 6
☎ 971 714610

San Lorenzo €€€

This charming six-room 17th-century mansion, located in the historic old town, has been restored with care to create a home away from home, except that parking is a challenge. There's no lift but a rope and pulley can hoist your luggage up to the third floor. The little breakfast room with the art deco bar imported from Paris is a great place to start the day, while the roof-top swimming-pool and garden provide a delightful oasis after a hard day's sightseeing.

➕ 176 B3 ✉ Carrer Sant Llorenç 14
☎ 971 728200; fax: 971 711901;
email: info@hotelsanlorenzo.com;
www.hotelsanlorenzo.com

Where to... Eat and Drink

Prices

The € amount indicates what you can expect to pay per person for a meal, excluding drinks, tax and tip. € = under 15 Euros €€ = 15–30 Euros €€€ = over 30 Euros

Haute cuisine here, from both land and sea, is determined largely by the season, by the harvest, by the morning market, so don't expect spring lamb in summer! Guinea fowl on the winter menu is replaced in summer with marinated tuna salad. The springtime creamy asparagus and almond soup is likely to be replaced by a wild mushroom pastry in autumn. The restaurant listings below are merely guidelines as to the kind of food and service to expect: there are many others to try.

Can Joan de s'Aigo €

Although the other locale, in the historic quarter, has been serving coffee for 300 years, this branch has a brighter mood. Red velvet chairs and banquettes, damask drapes, gilded mirrors on the walls and copper pots here and there reflect the light from the lacy chandeliers overhead. The *café con leche* is so good it's almost a meal, especially when downed with a golden *ensaimada* (sweet pastry) dusted with powdered sugar; *ensaimadas* are freshly baked all day long. The hot chocolate, the cold, sweet almond milk and the light almond

ice-cream are legendary. The original establishment sold ice, primarily for medicinal purposes, brought down in winter from the mountains. The almond cake is made the old-fashioned way with no flour, only almonds, sugar and egg whites.

➕ 176 B4 ✉ Baró Santa Maria del Sepulcre 5 ☎ 971 725760
🕐 Wed–Mon 8 am–9 pm

Celler Sa Premsa €

At Sa Premsa, the dust of decades decorates garlic braids and large gourds on the walls, the high ceilings, the overhead fans and the great oak wine barrels that circle the room, but people come for the crowded, noisy and dusty milieu, reminiscent of an old-fashioned boarding house where everyone sits on benches at long tables. The food is traditional Mallorcan, with country bread and tart, green olives as starters. The french fries are crisp and the croquettes melt in your mouth. Although the house speciality is pork loin with cabbage, there is a mouth-watering choice of dishes.

🚹 177 D5 ⊠ Plaça Bisbe Berenguer de Palou 8 ☎ 971 723529 ⏰ Mon–Sat 12:30–4, 7:30–11:30

El Café €€

The dining-room is simple, modern and elegant with white marble floors and a wall of glass looking out to the pavement tables. The lunch-time *menu del día* might include a rice salad, breaded and fried sole, with a chocolate brownie for dessert. A la carte options include artichoke-stuffed ravioli with pesto sauce, green beans with duck liver pâté, and the dessert special comprising vanilla and chocolate ice-cream. This is also a popular place to meet for drinks or afternoon tea. Iced tea and iced coffee are popular summer coolers.

🚹 177 D3 ⊠ Plaça Weyler 3 (in the Gran Hotel) ☎ 971 728077 ⏰ Mon–Sat 9–9, Sun 10–2

Es Baluard €€€

This restaurant, just around the corner from the San Lorenzo Hotel (▶ 60), is owned and operated by Joan Torrens Cantallops from the family that run Can Amer in Inca, so you know the food has got to be good. Here is first-class modern Mallorcan cuisine, perfectly cooked. The mushrooms stuffed with seafood are delectable, and so is the lamb shoulder stuffed with *sobrasada* (pork sausage spread) and aubergines. The wine menu offers a wide selection at acceptable prices, but the robust house red is fine. The décor is Mallorcan and each table is decorated with a single orange as big as a grapefruit, while artistic harvest displays of fruits and vegetables are placed around the L-shaped room. Brightly coloured ceramic plates, common in island kitchens, decorate the walls, with a shelf of antique demitasses behind the bar.

🚹 176 B3 ⊠ Plaça Porta Santa Catalina 9 ☎ 971 719609 ⏰ Mon–Sat 1–4, 8–11:30

Fábrica 23 €€

This popular restaurant in the buzzing Santa Catalina district is run by British chef Alexei Tarsey and his brother Sascha. The food is modern Mediterranean with eclectic influences ranging from Italy to the Far East. Get here early for the great-value lunch-time set menu, which includes water and wine. The evening menu changes daily according to what is in the market and is chalked up in Spanish on a blackboard, but might include celery, apple and roquefort soup, duck breast with five spices and mango sorbet for dessert.

🚹 176 A4 ⊠ Carrer Fábrica 23 ☎ 971 453125 ⏰ Tue–Sat 1–3:30, 9–11:30

Jarana €€

Jarana is tucked away in the Palma neighbourhood where fishermen and their families used to live. Currently fashionable because of its proximity to the port, the area is being renovated. Here is Madrid food at its best, especially the savoury and filling *cocido madrileño* (Madrid stew), lunch-time speciality of the house, but there is a full menu to choose from. Try the *patatas bravas* (spiced chunks of fried potatoes), the creamy leek soup and the ratatouille with pork loin. The pears in red wine make a tasty but light dessert.

🚹 176 A4 ⊠ Carrer Cotoner 47 ☎ 971 455628 ⏰ Daily 1:3–3:30, 8–12, except Wed and Sun evening

Koldo Royo €€€

Try to ignore the terrible paintings on the walls because the real art is on the plates. Creative Basque chef Koldo Royo has created a brilliant gourmet sampling menu of palate-tickling mini-portions (*menu degustacio*), which might read something like this: oyster salad with seawater sherbet, duck soup with mushrooms and corn, sea bass on a bed of black sepia pasta, oxtail stuffed with pig's trotters, and cheese and quince tart with ice-cream; it's all delicious and surprisingly light. The lightly breaded baked catch of the day is also exquisite. Local executives, lawyers and politicians keep coming back for the reasonably priced lunch-time *menú del día*, but staff neglect to tell newcomers about this bargain, so be sure to ask. Prices go up for the evening meal. Request a window table for the wonderful view of Palma harbour when you reserve; there's a comfortable lounge downstairs if you have to wait. For the chef's secrets, buy his cookery book on your way out.

➕ 176 off A3 ⊠ Passeig Marítim 3
☎ 971 732435; www.koldoroyo.es
🕐 Opening times vary in summer and winter – book ng essential

La Bóveda €

The best tapas bar in Palma has wine barrels for tables and a lovely old tiled bar. Choose from plates of ham or sausages, *tortilla* (potato omelette), seafood croquettes or specialities such as dates wrapped in bacon or spicy Galician peppers. The

pa amb oli (bread with olive oil and tomato) with ham makes a complete meal. A newer version of the same restaurant, Taberna la Bóveda, is just around the corner with tables on a seafront terrace in summer.

➕ 176 B2 ⊠ Carrer Boteria 3
☎ 971 714863
🕐 Mon–Sat 1:30–4, 8:30–12:30

La Locanda Umbra €€

It's worth coming here if only for the visual feast of the central round table laden with dozens of appetisers vaying from grilled and marinated aubergine to small stuffed squid. The price is determined by the size of the plate you choose. Try the home-made gnocchi with prawns and wild mushrooms, the breaded veal cutlet with tomato, garlic and rosemary, and possibly the tiramisu for dessert. Most diners are Palmesaños who like the friendly service and the good food at reasonable prices.

➕ 176 off A3 ⊠ Carrer Torrent 4
☎ 971 453623 🕐 Mon–Fri 1–3,45, 8–11:45, Sat 8–11:45

L@ Red Cybercafé €

This is what a cybercafé should be: a dozen computer stations with fast connections, lively background music, games like Parcheesi and Trivial Pursuit, newspapers and computer magazines in several languages, a tasty quiche lorraine and a variety of sandwiches, fresh orange juice and banana milkshakes, and numerous brands of beer. The mood of the Information Age is set by the clocks of five time zones, the satellite receivers overhead and a Planet Earth globe hanging over the computer terminals.

➕ 176 C4 ⊠ Concepció 5
☎ 971 713574; 🕐 Mon–Fri 10 am–1 am, Sat–Sun 5 pm–1 am

La Taberna del Caracol €

Food and service are impeccable at this little gem tucked into the old quarter near the Arab Baths (▶ 55). Halogen track lighting creates a cosy mood in spite of the high walls with high-level windows. Hanging braids of red peppers and

tomatoes, jars of marinating olives, terracotta jugs with little trays at the bottom for hens to drink from and the open kitchen make this a favourite. The warm chicken livers with lettuce salad are absolutely scrumptious. The lunch-time three-course *menú del día* is one of the best bargains in the city in the light and flavour department. Come early or late if you don't want to wait.

➕ 177 E2 ⊠ Sant Alonso 2
☎ 971 714908 🕐 Mon–Sat 1–3.30, 7:30–11:30

Parlament €€

This is a great place to enjoy a quick paella and they'll even make it for one person. Rice with squid, tinted black by the ink, is another favourite, or ask about the daily special. It's very busy at lunch-time with government workers, politicians and journalists, so either reserve a table or plan to take a longer lunch break and enjoy a lengthy aperitif at the bar. The friendly waiters in their black waistcoats, bustling about, seem to suit the Victorian décor with its big crystal chandeliers, and gilded mirrors framed with wood panelling.

➕ 176 C3 ✉ Conquistador 11
☎ 971 726026 🕐 Mon–Sat 1–4:30, 7:30–12:30, Sun 1–4:30

Vecchio Giovanni €

The colourful cockerel overhead in front announces this restaurant with five dining areas and 100 different dishes. Vegetarians like the wild mushrooms in creamed garlic, the cauliflower au gratin and the baked aubergines with red peppers and tomatoes. Portions are generous and service is friendly. A bas-relief of *The Last Supper* dominates one wall of the main dining-room; much of the other artwork is by Julio Viera, a student of Salvador Dalí.

➕ 176 C3 ✉ Carrer San Juan 3
☎ 971 72879
🕐 Tue–Sun 1–3, 6:30–11:30

Where to... Shop

Palma continues to be the commercial capital of the island and you can shop until you drop in the old quarter, in the city centre, in shopping centres or in the suburbs. And there are markets in Plaça Major on Monday and Friday mornings.

Porto Pi Shopping Centre

This huge complex, located at the west end of the Passeig Marítim, has more than 100 shops and 1,500 free parking spaces all under one roof. Shops are open from Monday to Saturday 10 am to 10 pm and are grouped vaguely by area: clothes, shoes and accessories; speciality shops and services; home furnishings and gifts. **Artesanos Camiseros**, which boasts 150 shops around the world, stocks 300 fabrics and can hand-tailor a shirt or blouse to order in four days. **Mercat Artesà**, hiding under the escalator, has exquisite Carnival-of-Venice leather masks and chess sets with traditional Mallorcan farmworkers as pieces. **Bibliono Papeleria** sells lovely handmade wrapping paper and little spring-launched flying butterflies, among other things. At **Viajes Y Aventura**, you can pick up a Swiss army knife, a collapsible cane for hiking or a Coleman gas camping lamp and, in case you've lapsed into a shopping coma, an extra suitcase to carry everything home. For fuel, you'll find an enormous supermarket, several ice-cream parlours and fast-food outlets.

El Corte Inglés

Although the streets of Palma are lined with thousands of shops, Avinguda Jaime III and the neighbouring side streets are favourites. You'll enjoy strolling along and browsing under the arcades, but one of best places to buy is **El Corte Inglés** (Avinguda Jaume III, 15 and Avinguda d'Alexandre Roselló, 12; www.elcorteingles.es), one of Spain's best department stores. You can do almost all your holiday shopping here: there is a wide selection of goods, fair prices and personable staff. The Gourmet Club deli stocks around 1,000 wines, a range of olive oils, sausages and cheeses, picnic packs for a day on the beach, and numerous other gastronomic delights. There is also a full supermarket and cafeteria. Clothing for youngsters and adults sport many designer labels. Fashion accessories include stylish leather wallets, bags and backpacks. There is an electronics shop, a bookshop, a film processing counter, and underground parking. If you make a purchase of more than 90 and are a resident of a non-EU country, you can get the IVA sales tax refunded when you leave Spain: El Corte Inglés takes care of most of the paperwork.

Where to...
Be Entertained

There's so much to do in Palma: to find out what's on, pick up *The Reader* or *Majorca Daily Bulletin* English-language newspapers at your hotel desk or the nearest news-stand.

Helicopter Flights

Sloane Helicopters offers flying lessons and pleasure flights, with magnificent aerial views of the island. During an introductory half-hour lesson you will be encouraged to take the controls. If you just want to sit back and let someone else do the work, you can book a one-hour pleasure flight for around €450. Contact Sloane Helicopters Mallorca at Son Bonet aerodrome (tel: 971 794132; email: info@sloanemallorca.com; www.sloanemallorca.com).

Concerts and Theatre

Music concerts, theatre, ballet and opera are held regularly at the Auditorium (Passeig Marítim 18; tel: 971 734735). The 19th-century Teatre Principal (Plaça Weyler; tel: 971 713356; website: www.teatreprincipal.com) showcases fine opera and theatre.

Cinema

Although Palma has numerous cinemas, the Renoir (S'Escorxador, Emperatriz Eugenia 6; tel: 971 205408) shows films in their original language with Spanish subtitles. The admission price includes two hours of free parking.

Night-life

Mediterranean summer nights are so lovely, little wonder no one wants to sleep. The area around Plaça Llotja is lively until after midnight. Abaco (Carrer Sant Joan) provides the most luxurious mood for an evening drink. You open a massive wooden door and step inside a 17th-century mansion furnished with sumptuous antiques, a cornucopia of fruits and vegetables, arrangements of flowers and foliage, and candles large and small by the dozens, while Chopin and other Classics waft through the air. La Bóveda (▶ 62) serves numerous *tapas* and several variations of *pa amb oli*. To watch the moon rise over Palma Bay, go down to the docks where city and sea meet to the waterfront terraces of the Puerto Pesquero or Dàrsena bars (both along the Passeig Marítim). After midnight, young people often move on for disco at Lluna or Pacha (both along the Passeig Marítim), jazz (Bar Barcelona; Apuntadores 5) or blues (Blues Ville; Carrer Ma d'es Moro 3). The Café Restaurant Real (Avinguda Gabriel Alomar y Villalonga 11) is open 24 hours a day. For a Las Vegas-style show and dinner, go either to the Casino or Son Amar (Carretera de Soller, Km 10.8; tel: 971 617533; website: www.sonamar.com), where you might find Celtic dancers, the Spanish Ballet, The Drifters or the Angelo Magic Show.

Spectator Sports

Bullfighting, which is more pageantry than sport, takes place on Sunday afternoons at the Plaça de Toros (Avinguda Gaspar B Arquitecte 32; tel: 971 755245) from April to October. It's advisable to pay extra for a seat in the shade. You may not appreciate the pride and passion: it's been a Spanish tradition for more than a millennium, but is now gradually being replaced by football. There are frequent football matches at various stadiums around the city.

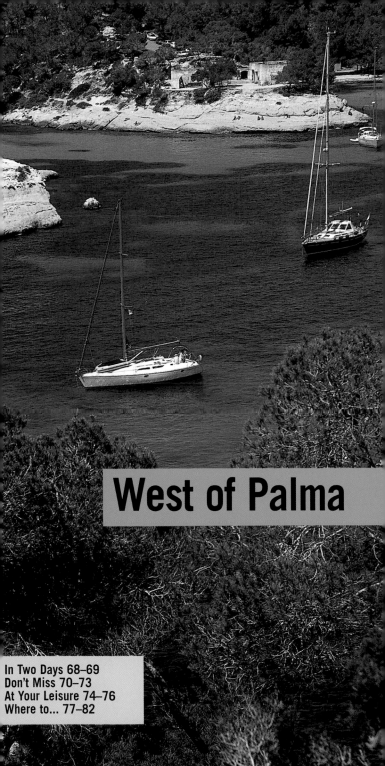

West of Palma

Getting Your Bearings

The west side of the island is Mallorca in miniature, with bustling resorts, beautiful bays and coves, a wild northern coastline and spectacular mountain scenery. This was the first part of Mallorca to be developed for tourism and the construction crane has been an inescapable part of the landscape for almost half a century. Quiet fishing villages have been turned into bucket-and-spade resorts and the coastline has been disfigured by soulless apartment blocks and hotels. Fortunately, the Mallorcans are now learning from the mistakes of the past; new building is carefully controlled and the worst offenders are being dismantled to make way for stylish, palm-lined promenades.

Around the Bay of Palma, millionaires rub shoulders with taxi-drivers as chichi marinas exist side by side with crowded holiday beaches. Despite the downmarket reputation of resorts such as Magaluf, this area has always held an appeal for the fashionable and super-rich. King Juan Carlos and Queen Sofía of Spain spend their summers in residence at Marivent, the pink palace perched on a cliff in Cala Major. Film stars moor their yachts at nearby

Punta des Fabioler

Cap Tramuntana

Sa Dragonera

9

Cap des Llebeig

▲ Puig de Sa Trapa

8 Sant Elm

S'Arracó
○
PM103
An

C7

Port d'Andratx
7
Cala

Cala d'Egos

Cap de sa Mola

Cap des Llamp
A

The sun setting over the sea at Sant Elm is one of the most memorable Mallorcan moments

Page 65:
Portals Vells –
an idyllic spot

★ Don't Miss

At Your Leisure

Puerto Portals. The racing driver Michael Schumacher and the model Claudia Schiffer are just two of those to have bought luxury villas in fashionable Camp de Mar.

Away from the coast, life goes on as it always has, in market towns like Andratx and sleepy villages like Puigpunyent, where the biggest excitement is the olive harvest and the predominent sound is the tinkling of sheep-bells on the hillside. Even on the coast, you sometimes discover an unexpected pocket of peace where you can get away from it all. A beautiful walking and cycling trail, lit up at night, borders the road from Portals Nous to Palma Nova, not far from the bronzed bodies and pounding discos of Magaluf.

This two-day circuit of western Mallorca
takes in crowded beaches, glitzy resorts and the dramatic
scenery of the north coast.

West of Palma in Two Days

Day 1

Morning

Head out from Palma on the coast road, passing the King's summer palace at Cala Major. If you enjoy surrealist art, an essential detour here is to the Fundació Pilar i Joan Miró (▶ 74), where the Catalan painter Joan Miró lived and worked for the last 27 years of his life. Continue to Portals Nous and stroll around Puerto Portals (pictured below, ▶ 70), looking out for minor royals and dreaming of winning the lottery. Alternatively, if you have children, take in one of the dolphin shows at Marineland (pictured right, ▶ 74).

Afternoon

Time for an afternoon on the beach – just take your pick (▶ 72). Families will enjoy Palma Nova, which has plenty of sand and excellent facilities. After lunch, stroll around the headland to Magaluf to see some of the worst excesses of mass tourism. For something a bit quieter, drive through the pine woods to Portals Vells.

Evening

Discover the bars and discos of Magaluf, such as BCM Disco Empire (▶ 82). It may not be everyone's cup of tea (or pint of lager), but it's an essential Mallorca experience.

Day 2

Morning

Drive to Andratx (above, ➤ 75) and take the side road to Sant Elm (➤ 75) for views of Sa Dragonera (➤ 76) from the beach. In summer you can take a boat trip for a close-up look at the island. Afterwards, enjoy a seafood lunch at one of the restaurants on the jetty with Sa Dragonera as a backdrop.

Afternoon

Return to Andratx and follow signs for Estellencs for a spectacular drive along the northwest coast. The road twists and turns between the pine woods and the cliffs, with *miradors* where you can pause to admire the sea views. Eventually you arrive in Banyalbufar, a small village with terraced hillsides sloping down to the sea. Beyond Banyalbufar, a right turn leads to La Granja (regular traditional music sessions, right, ➤ 76), a good place to gain an insight into rural Mallorcan traditions. From here, a narrow road snakes through the mountains, passing the little village of Puigpunyent, the entry point for La Reserva (➤ 168). The road continues to Galilea, a hilltop village, then tumbles down the hillside towards Calvià, an ordinary country town which just happens to be the municipality that contains Puerto Portals, Palma Nova and Magaluf.

Puerto Portals

This luxury marina, just down the cliff from
Portals Nous, is the summer capital of Mallorca's
jet set. Celebrities, fashion icons and members
of the Spanish royal family all moor their yachts
here, in a privileged position on Palma Bay.

Built in 1986, the port, thanks to its impressive infrastructure,
has attracted the rich and famous from numerous nations and
has become the centre for several important sailing events; if
you stroll along the docks, you will see many different flags
flying. There are often boats for sale, and someone is always
scrubbing a deck or polishing brass or chrome.

The marina waterfront promenade has become a place to see
and be seen. Classy restaurants, cafés and bars like Tristán
(► 80), one of the royal family's breakfast spots, and the
Squadron Sports Café (► 80), a favourite with serious sailors,
line the dockfront. The passing fashion parade could compete
with the Champs-Elysées in Paris; some of the designer outfits
may have been purchased in the neighbouring high-priced
boutiques. Occasionally someone turns a table into an instant
office, complete with briefcase, newspapers, notebooks, charts
and a mobile phone in constant use. Well-cared-for canines
roam around to meet and greet, while sparrows perch on chair-
backs and sun umbrellas waiting for crumbs to fall. Beyond the
passing parade of delivery trucks, cars and other vehicles, sleek
white motor cruisers gleam in the sunshine. The square white
tower with various antennae reaching up from the tiled roof is
the Captain's Tower, site of the port's administrative offices and

Stylish Puerto Portals is the St Tropez of Mallorca

Warm sea breezes make the island a popular sailing centre

✚ 178 C1
✉ Palma Nova Tourist Office, Passeig de la Mar 13 ☎ 971 682365
🚌 20, 21, 22 from Palma to Portals Nous

the international symbol of Puerto Portals.

On the waterfront and the street behind, you will also find a bank, a travel agency, car and boat hire offices, a sailing school, supermarket, newsagents, discotheque and, in case you want to stay longer, estate agents and yacht brokers.

TAKING A BREAK

The most interesting spot to have a drink is likely to be an outdoor table at Wellies (➤ 81). Stop for a morning coffee and croissant with fresh orange juice.

PUERTO PORTALS: INSIDE INFO

Top tip For those who want to sunbathe, just beyond the shipyard at the east end of the shopping area is the small stretch of sandy beach, frequented mostly by residents and boat crews. The beach is fairly sheltered and a real suntrap on cooler days. From here, it's a short swim out to the little Illa d'en Sales, where a path leads up to the top of the island.
• If you feel like walking, stroll along the high concrete breakwater around the harbour and climb up the cliff from the harbour to the village centre of Portals Nous, which has a string of restaurants, bars, cafés, and a bookshop stocked with a wide range of books in English.

Hidden gem A short distance south of the Portals Nous taxi stand is the American School. But the real reason for heading in this direction is the terrace of the little oratory Nostra Senyora de Portals, ideal for renewing your wedding vows, at the end of the street. From here, you can look down to a splendid view of Puerto Portals and all around the bay.

Beaches

The nearest beaches to Palma are at Cala Major and Sant Agustí. At one time these were separate resorts, but they have expanded to become virtually suburbs of Palma and it is difficult to tell where one ends and the next begins.

Sant Agustí

At the T-junction with traffic lights, turn left into the Calanova sailing school with its small yacht harbour. You should be able to find a parking place here, then you can explore on foot. One great spot is about 100m east, just after La Trattoria, where a sign points south to "Huckleberrys". Walk down a few steps to the terrace where there is a large palm tree for shade. Here is an oasis of calm in a busy neighbourhood, and short paths lead to rocks where you can sunbathe and down to the water if you want to swim.

TAKING A BREAK

For the price of a coffee, you can swim in Huckleberry's pool; the food is quite good and reasonably priced, so you may also want to stay for lunch (► 79).

Ses Illetes

About 7km from Palma is a peninsula with three small islands offshore. You can take a boat trip from the Hotel Bonanza whose lobby has a stunning sea view. Parking can be a problem, however, so unless you're staying at one of the several good hotels in Ses Illetes, a better bet is a kilometre or so further west. Follow the signs to the charming Hotel Bendinat and park on the street. The rocks outside the fence in front of the hotel are a wonderful spot for sunbathing and snorkelling. The main beach at Ses Illetes gets very crowded at weekends with sun worshippers from Palma, but a walk of around 1km leads to a second beach on the edge of the resort.

Visitors have always loved the broad sandy beach at Palma Nova

Portals Nous/Puerto Portals (► 70)

Palma Nova

Palma Nova has shallow water with a long beach of fine sand backed by a heavily commercialised promenade lined with shops, eateries and English bars. The resort is crowded and very popular

🕂 178 C1

🚌 There are regular buses to all these beaches from Palma, except Portals Vells which can only be reached by car

with families. For outdoor action, there is water-skiing and paragliding. A short walk around the headlands leads past a second beach to Magaluf, the biggest and brashest resort in Palma Bay. The beach here is superb, activities range from windsurfing to boat trips, but the riotous night-life will not appeal to everyone.

TAKING A BREAK

Caesar's is great for seafood specials and Grand Café Cappuccino is a popular place with a nice atmosphere for coffee. A bonus is the overhead gas heaters for alfresco winter meals on the terrace.

The midday *menú del día* at the Mesón Son Caliu (➤ 79) is one of the best value-for-money establishments on the island.

BEACHES: INSIDE INFO

Top tips The larger beaches, such as Palma Nova, Magaluf and Peguera, have **first-aid stations** and **warning flags** which alert you to unsafe conditions. Keep an eye on young children and never let them go near the sea if the red or yellow warning flags are flying.

• Continue past Portals Vells to the headland of Cala Figuera for the **best views** of Palma Bay.

Portals Vells

Located on a pine-studded peninsula, Portals Vells has several secluded coves with sandy beaches, including the tiny nudist beach of Platja Mago, that have become quite popular with an up-market villa crowd. A path carved into the rock leads to an abandoned quarry (some of the stone was used to build Palma Cathedral) with a cave church, although the venerated statue of the Virgin Mary that once was here has been moved to a chapel in Portals Nous for safekeeping.

A cave in Portals Vells was turned into a church by shipwrecked sailors from Genoa who carved an altar into the rock

Santa Ponça

At Santa Ponça, a tall white cross marks the spot where Christian conqueror Jaume I stepped ashore in 1229. German tourists discovered this broad sandy beach, 0.5km long with shallow water, and developers turned it into a mega-resort. However, there is still a lovely pine grove on the beachfront. You can take a boat with an underwater window to nearby Malgrat Island (El Malgrat), while another boat sails regularly to Sa Dragonera, Sant Elm and Port d'Andratx.

Peguera

There is a splendid promenade which runs past the big hotels and along three broad sandy beaches. A kilometre west is Cala Fornells, a small beach backdropped with low-rise villas climbing up the steep slopes above the bay.

At Your Leisure

1 Fundació Pilar i Joan Miró

Even those who do not like modern art are enthralled by Joan Miró, the Catalan artist whose primary colours and bright surrealist designs seem to capture the Mediterranean light. Born in Barcelona, Miró spent his childhood holidays in Mallorca and lived here from 1956 until his death in 1983. His studio remains much as it was with unfinished canvases and half-empty cans of paint. Some 6,000 of his paintings, sketches, engravings, murals, sculptures and installations are on display. The Foundation is a cultural centre with ongoing exhibitions, concerts and conferences and has an art library and a cafeteria.

➕ 179 D2 ✉ Joan de Saridakis 29, Cala Major
☎ 971 701420 🕐 Tue–Sat 10–6 (10–7 mid-May–mid-Sep), Sun 10–3
🚌 3,6 from Palma 💲 Moderate

Joan Miró's simple spots and lines inspire the imagination

5 Nemo Submarine

If you're looking for soft aquatic adventure but don't want to get wet, shake the sand off your shoes and head for Magaluf and the Nemo, a kind of submergible bus, almost as comfortable as your living room. The white sub drifts slowly down underwater for a fish-eye view of the bottom of the Med, a memory-of-a-lifetime experience.

A motorboat picks you up on the dock and takes you out to the waiting sub near an island 1km offshore. The Finnish-made submarine, designed for tourism, carries 46 passengers and a crew of two. Passengers sit in pairs on soft leather stools in front of a round metre-wide porthole. Each of the 22 viewing stations sports an instrument panel where green lights indicate depth, direction, speed, water temperature and above-sea conditions, and a card illustrates various fish that you might see through your porthole. It's easy to take good photos, since the windows are spotlessly clean, there is ample room for angle shots, and the sunshine from above shines down through the water. Nemo glides past several old shipwrecks for a close-up view. A Nemo scuba-diver points out such creatures of the deep as octopus and starfish. The Nemo gift shop sells videos, photos, T-shirts and other souvenirs of your underwater adventure.

➕ 178 C1 ✉ Carrer Galeon 2, Magaluf ☎ 971 130244;

3 Marineland

Several excellent shows daily star the endearing aquatic aerobics of dolphins and sea lions while another set of shows features chatty, colourful and versatile cycling parrots. Judging from audience response, each show is better than the other. Marineland, which sits on the coast opposite the Punta Negra Hotel, also has various aquarium displays, a colony of Emperor penguins and a reptile community.

➕ 178 C1 ✉ Costa d'en Blanes
☎ 971 675125
🕐 Daily 9:30–7, Apr–Sep; 9:30–5, Oct–Dec and Feb–Mar; closed Jan
💲 Expensive

fax: 971 130229;
email:
info@nemosub.com;
www.nemosub.com ⏰ Tue–Sat 9–8,
Apr–Oct 💰 Expensive

6 Andratx

Surrounded by almond groves and
orange orchards in the foothills of the
Tramuntana, Andratx is a typical
Mallorcan town which springs to life
on Wednesdays when the streets fill
with tour buses for the weekly market.
The Romans had a town here known
as *Andrachium*, and when King Jaume
I conquered Mallorca, he made his
home here. The highlight of the town
is the 13th-century church of Santa
Maria which also doubled as a watch-
tower and fortress in medieval times
when pirates were a problem. You may
enjoy a quiet stroll through the old
cobbled streets any day of the week.
➕ 178 B2

7 Port d'Andratx

This old fishing port has become a
bustling resort of apartments, hotels,
homes, restaurants and first-rate
shops creeping inland and up the
slopes flanking the long rectangular
bay. The German deli in the centre
of the shopping area on the south
side of the harbour is a good place
to pick up a picnic, and the look-out
site at the tip of the southside

**Port d'Andratx is typical of the many
bustling commercial and pleasure ports
along Mallorca's coastline**

peninsula is the best
spot to watch the sun
set at sea.
➕ 178 B2

8 Sant Elm

Sant Elm,
40km from
Palma by
road, is to
Mallorca what
Land's End is to
England – the west-
ernmost tip of the
island. The twisting road
in from Andratx ends at a
delightful small beach,
skirted with rocky coves ideal
for underwater exploration. Local
outfitters organise scuba-diving
excursions among the submerged,
craggy rocks and windsurfing and
water-skiing. If you like sailing, you
will love the stiff breezes offshore.
Sant Elm is also the starting point
for a hike up the well-trodden trail

towards Puig de Sa Trapa. Although fire razed 800ha of forest around the trail in 1994, reforestation was completed in 2000.

The Restaurant Sant Elm (➤ 80) near the dock is the spot to sit back and suck in the surrounding scenery.

➕ 178 A2

❾ Sa Dragonera

Rearing out of the sea like a benign 4-km long dragon, about 1km offshore from Sant Elm is Sa Dragonera, the southwest tip of the Tramuntana. Since 1995, this chunk of rock has been a protected park, popular with nature lovers. The trail that links the dock with the light-house on the south end of the island overlooks the coast. Ferries run several times a day from Sant Elm on excursions around the island to explore the peaceful coves and trails. You will see cormorants, gulls and sea eagles wheeling overhead, and maybe even an Eleonora's falcon.

➕ 178 A2 ☎ 971 180632 (park); 971 757061 (boat trips, Mar–Oct) ⏰ Daily 10–3 💷 Free (park); expensive (boat trips

Redbeard, the 15th-century pirate, chose rocky Sa Dragonera as a home base

❿ La Granja

This grand old farm, set in a magnificent mountain valley, is fun to visit in spite of its popularity. The spring water here has been important since Roman times and supplies the

Traditional dancing is demonstrated at La Granja

neighbouring village of Esporles. The fountain at the end of the garden spouts 9m upwards like a geyser, directly from its subterranean source. Once a Moorish farm, later a Cistercian convent, La Granja is again a farm, but now a commercial operation open to the public. Intriguing displays vary from a collection of Inquisition torture instruments to a fully furnished baroque bedroom and bathroom to a forest of small deer. During craft displays you can help yourself to wines and juices and sample such traditional Mallorcan snacks as spinach pizza and figcakes while a musician in medieval Mallorcan costume plays goatskin bagpipes. Shaded by a 1,000-year-old yew tree, you can watch an instrumental quartet and folk-dancers perform on stage in the garden, backdropped by a pond of splashing ducks and a field of grazing sheep.

➕ 178 C3 ✉ Carretera Esporles-Puigpunyent, Km 2, Esporles ☎ 971 610032; fax: 971 619305; email: info@lagranja.net; www.lagranja.net ⏰ Daily 10–7, Apr–Sep; 10–6, rest of year. Craft displays Wed and Fri 3:30–5 💷 Expensive

Where to... Stay

Prices

Prices are for the least expensive double room in high season, IVA sales tax included. Prices may drop by up to 50 per cent in low season. Breakfast is usually included in the room price. € = under 60 Euros €€ = 60–120 Euros €€€ = over 120 Euros

This region west of Palma is the busiest tourism area on the island and can provide almost anything you could ask for in terms of accommodation and complementary services.
Hotels are reasonably priced and many stay open throughout the year.

Bendinat Golf €€€

Located in the middle of the golf-course of the same name, this luxurious hotel caters for golfers, as well as the youngish *movida* crowd; staff wear golf-shirts and no ties, and continental breakfast is available until 1 pm. The 101 bright and airy guest rooms and suites are housed in three low-rise buildings fronted with New Orleans-style latticed balconies. Dark wood lines the lobby lounge which is decorated like a safari hotel in Kenya. The fitness centre comprises indoor and outdoor swimming-pools, a whirlpool bath, colour therapy sauna, Turkish steam bath, Kneipp hydrotherapy, solarium and massage rooms.

🚹 178 C2 ✉ Avinguda Bendinat 58, Portals Nous
☎ 971 675725; fax: 971 677276;
email: info@hotelbendinat.es;
www.hotelbendinat.es

Hostal La Mimosa €

La Mimosa is a lovely renovated villa within walking distance of three beaches and the Calanova Sailing School, yet is only a ten-minute drive from the city centre and a five-minute drive from the Bendinat Golf Club west. All 18 rooms are equipped with private bath. Be sure to request a sea view or one of the garden terrace rooms near the swimming-pool. The lounge has a widescreen TV, table tennis and darts, with occasional live evening entertainment and barbecues by the pool bar. You can check your email or log on to the web (for a fee) at the computer in the bar.

🚹 179 D2 ✉ Carrer Suecia 5, Sant Agusti ☎ 971 400101;
fax: 971 707584.
www.mallorca2000.com/lamimosa

Punta Negra €€€

A gracious old hotel, the Punta Negra is a pocket of peace in a region of hustle and bustle. Its a 20-minute stroll east along the promenade to Puerto Portals and 20 minutes west to Palma Nova. There are four golf-courses in the immediate area. Thanks to its peninsula location, most rooms sport a sea view through luxuriant pines which attract sparrows and hoopoes while seagulls glide on the offshore air currents. The barking you hear in the evening is the sea lions at Marineland across the cove. Beyond the swimming-pool, a trail leads down to two small secluded sandy beaches. The rocky regions underwater provide good snorkelling. The lobby lounge has a big open fireplace where the olive-wood fire is one of the best-kept secrets of winter in Mallorca.

🚹 178 C1 ✉ Carretera Andratx, Km 12, Costa d'en Blanes ☎ 971 680762;
fax: 971 683319;
email: hpuntanegra@terre.es;
www.hotelpuntanegra.com

Son Caliu Hotel €€€

This Best Western calls itself "Mallorca's friendliest hotel" and it is. The staff are concerned about your happiness and comfort but don't

Where to...
Eat and Drink

Prices

The € amount indicates what you can expect to pay per person for a meal, excluding drinks, tax and tip. € = under 15 Euros €€ = 15–30 Euros €€€ = over 30 Euros

Bar del Titanic €

This is a great place to drop anchor for a few hours and enjoy some *tapas*, the house speciality. Whether you eat and drink inside or out, the best item to order is the assortment plate, which comes with six small portions of potato and onion omelette, baby herrings marinated in oil and garlic, beef and pork meat balls, mini-sausages, chicken wings and potato salad. Decorative memorabilia include an intriguing collection of postcards mailed from the *Titanic*, two models of the luxury liner, the lunch

menu from that fatal day (12 April, 1912), the full-page cover-age from the *New York Times*, and beautiful souvenir coasters with an artistic rendering of the ship and the iceberg.

➕ 178 C1 ⊠ Puerto Portals
☎ 971 677345 🕐 10 am–late

Cappuccino Grand Café €

Hot, black and sweet: that's how the Spanish like their coffee; the Palma Nova Cappuccino Café is more mellow, even though the waiters are ultra-professional with their *fin de siècle* white shirts, black waistcoats, long wraparound

interfere. Situated in a small cove with a secluded beach and subtropical gardens centring around a shady rubber tree, this 230-room home-from-home has an outdoor pool, a large chlorine-free indoor pool (heated from Oct–May), a tennis-court, a beauty farm and entertainment in the lounge every evening. Children receive a 50 per cent discount. Dogs are welcome.

➕ 178 C1 ⊠ Urbanizacio Son Caliu, Palma Nova ☎ 971 682300; fax: 971 663720;
email: soncaliu@soncaliu.com; www.soncaliu.com

Son Malero €€

This renovated and restored *possessio*, dating from 1430, rests in a valley of almond and carob trees between the Tramuntana and the Na Burgesa hills, about 1km from Calvia. If you like painting, photography, walking or hiking, mountain biking, horse-riding, golf or simple solitude, this is a fine place to be. This agrotourism hotel

accommodates 12 people in four bedrooms, one studio and one apartment.

➕ 178 C2 ⊠ Camino Son Malero, Calvià ☎ 971 670301;
fax: 971 138018;
email: agroturismo@mallorcanet.com;
www.agroturismo-balear.com

Villamil €€€

In the centre of Peguera, the Hesperia Villamil Hotel is like a dream. At the front, stores and restaurants line the promenade (no traffic allowed after noon); at the back, sunny terraces and shady gardens (with romantic statues) spill down past the swimming-pool and tennis-court to a white sandy beach. The mood is elegant and relaxing. There is a restaurant on the terrace for summer dining. Most of the rooms have balconies and sea views; rooms at the back are cheaper.

➕ 178 B1 ⊠ Bulevar de Peguera 66, Peguera ☎ 971 686050; fax: 971 686815; email: reservas@hesperia-villamil.com; www.hesperia-villamil.com

white aprons and little round trays. Overhead halogen lights make the bottles behind the bar sparkle, while a display of fine china cups and saucers decorates the opposite wall. The liveliest time is around 6 pm on Sunday when local teenagers come to chat and play Scrabble, Tabu and dominoes. There are newspapers to read, parasailors and water-skiers to watch out for on the water, and heat on the outside terrace for damp days or evenings.

🔢 178 C1 ✉ Passeig del Mar 18, Palma Nova ☎ 971 681368 🕐 Daily 8:30 am–1 am

Ca Na Cuco €€

For classical Balearic cuisine, Ca Na Cuco almost matches Can Amer in Inca. The small menu changes with the season and the morning market. The thin and delicate but crispy wild asparagus of springtime is delightful. You can't go wrong with the fish soup or with the aubergines stuffed with prawns, mussels, monkfish and sepia. The dessert speciality is a frozen cake draped with chocolate sauce and crushed almonds. The view from the terrace is the imposing Calvià town hall across the road.

🔢 178 C2 ✉ Avinguda de Palma 14, Calvià ☎ 971 670083 🕐 Daily 12:30–3:30, 7–11

Club Nautico €€

This grill/cafeteria/bar/restaurant sports a super setting right inside the Santa Ponça Yacht Club, and you don't have to be a member to eat here. The *menú del día* (€) usually includes something like potato soup, loin of pork and sweet crêpes. There are tables inside, but most people prefer the deck tables overlooking the little fleet of moored yachts. While you're here, you might want to wander next door to the Liberian Motorboat & Yacht Club Inc. ("the love of liberty brought us here!") and sign up for a day and a half of jet-skiing. Or you may want to visit the park and

monument adjacent marking the spot where Christian conqueror Jaume I landed with his troops eight centuries ago.

🔢 178 C1 ✉ Via de la Cruz 46, Santa Ponça ☎ 971 690103 🕐 Thu–Tue 12–3, 7–11

Huckleberry's Beach Club €

A modest restaurant with a comfortable terrace shaded by a large palm tree, Huckleberry's is far enough from the street to be free of traffic noise. For the price of a Danish or Dutch open-sandwich and a beer, you can enjoy the swimming-pool and also have access to the sea.

🔢 179 D2 ✉ Carrer Joan Miró 305, Sant Agustí ☎ 971 702993 🕐 Daily 10 am–midnight (in summer)

La Hacienda €€

This Mexican ranch-style restaurant, right at the entrance to Peguera, is a refreshing change from the usual island fare. Try "La Hacienda Grande", a beef taco, chicken tortilla and cheese enchilada combo served with rice, beans, salad, guacamole and sour cream. The spare ribs with two sauces are also popular. The best drink with this, of course, is a marguerita, the house speciality. Colourfully decorated with sombreros, serapes and wagon wheels, La Hacienda makes you feel like you've been temporarily transported to Mexico.

🔢 178 B1 ✉ Pau Casals 1, Peguera ☎ 971 685473 🕐 Mon–Sat 5–midnight, Sun 1–midnight

Mesón Son Caliu €–€€

This has the best lunch-time meal for the price on the island. Food is fabulous, service is courteous and quick. A typical three-course meal might include rice broth with fish, stewed chicken with pine nuts, and flan or ice-cream for dessert. Hot homemade bread, green olives and table wine are included in the low-priced special. Specialities include snails in season, and wood-grilled suckling pig, kid and fish. The decor is rustic Mallorcan;

the summer bonus is the courtyard outside, while in winter there's a welcoming fire in the open fireplace inside.

➕ 178 C1 ✉ Carretera d'Andratx, Km 12, Son Caliu ☎ 971 680086 ⏰ Tue–Sun 1–4, 7–midnight

El Pescador €€

This deck overlooking the dock where the shuttle service to Sa Dragonera comes and goes is the best place to be for fish, seafood and setting. You can tell where the fish is fresh and good by where the cats are, and they are here. Owner/manager Damien is also the fisherman who brings in the catch of the day. You can even bring in your own catch of the day and they will grill it for you.

➕ 178 A2 ✉ Jaime I, 48, Sant Elm ☎ 971 239167 ⏰ Tue–Sun lunch and dinner

Restaurant Sporting Tenis €€

Located next door to Marineland, here you can feast on classic Mallorcan cuisine indoors or on the terrace with a view sweeping from the Captain's Tower at Puerto Portals westwards to the southernmost tip of the Calvià peninsula. The *menu del dia* (€) might feature a noodle paella, then creamed chicken, and ice-cream for dessert, or you can order grilled specialities like monkfish or suckling pig à la carte. If you overdo it, you can send the kids to the water-slide and hire a *chaise-longue* with an adjustable sunshade for the head, and siesta on the terrace. In case you're feeling energetic, you can play a set or two on one of seven clay tennis-courts (lit at night). There are also four table-tennis courts and a swimming-pool.

➕ 178 C1 ✉ Carretera d'Andratx, Km 10, Costa d'en Blanes ☎ 971 676456 ⏰ Tue–Sun 10 am–midnight

Rincón del Mar €

You can make lunch here part of a day at the beach, for Platja Son Caliu is one of the most delightful and accessible cosy patches of sand around. You can eat in the sun or in the shade of the striped marine blue-and-white awnings. For appetisers try the home-made spinach croquettes and, for the main course, you can choose from such dishes as shoulder of lamb, grilled swordfish, Hawaiian chicken and prawn curry. Remember to leave room for one of the dozens of Menorquina frozen desserts; everybody loves the lemon ice-cream frozen and served inside a real lemon. The Rincón del Mar may not win any grand culinary awards, but when the warm breeze whispers in through the palms and pines from the cerulean sea, you know that there is nowhere else in the world you'd rather be.

➕ 178 C1 ✉ Platja Son Caliu (just east of the Best Western Hotel) ☎ 971 681862 ⏰ Lunch and dinner daily

Squadron Sports Café €€

Sailors and other athletes like this fun-filled front-line café. The menu varies from burgers, salads, stroganoff and garlic prawns to the infamous Full Monty breakfast and the Sunday roast beef *menú del día*. Headquarters for several sports events throughout the year, the café offers such major spectator sporting events as football, rugby, tennis, cricket, powerboat and car racing – all on the big screen overhead. In case you want to check your email, there's a computer in the corner all hooked up and ready to read.

➕ 178 C1 ✉ Puerto Portals ☎ 971 677577 ⏰ Daily 8 am–10 pm

Tristán €€€

Tristán is top of the line in Mediterranean cuisine, thanks to innovative perfectionist chef Gerhard Schwaiger. You might want to try the crab gazpacho or the octopus with warm potato and pepper vinaigrette. But the polenta with black truffles and gruyère and the ravioli with fresh cheese and beef broth also receive high ratings. One of the most preferred desserts is crêpes with pineapple mousse and lemon ice-cream. The ambience is elegant and the service impeccable.

🖃 178 C1 ⊠ Puerto Portals ☎ 971 675547 🕐 Tue–Sun 8 pm–midnight

Wellies €€

Amiable and gently greying Geoffrey Kenion has been here for 14 years keeping customers happy, but it doesn't take much because the setting is so spectacular. Salads are as fresh as can be and the dressings delicate (except for the Caesar dressing which is exceptionally strong). The fried Brie is flavourful and so are the deep-fried morsels of monkfish with tartar sauce. If you're really hungry, go for roast duck or barbecued spare ribs with corn fritters. The rich and famous sometimes hide at the Top Deck upstairs, which is secluded, elegant and comfortable.

🖃 178 C1 ⊠ Puerto Portals ☎ 971 683898; fax: 971 681569 🕐 Daily 9 am–midnight

Where to... Shop

Like the rest of Mallorca, the area west of Palma has countless artisans skilled in working with wood, glass, clay, leather and other materials. So you will find attractive hand-crafted souvenirs for sale in urban areas from Sant Agustí to Calvià and Port d'Andratx.

Mercadona

On the eastern edge of Palma Nova, **Mercadona** covers a lot of territory and is a pleasant shopping centre. A gigantic supermarket sells everything from sangria to socks, while the foyer houses a fine jewellery stall and a bar/café with comfortable rattan chairs on the terrace. A news kiosk sells international newspapers and magazines as well as odds and ends from stationery to backpacks. **Stadium Sport** has just about everything you need for an active life outdoors or for the gym upstairs. The **Around The World** store sells everything from designer candles to Italian silks and Indian cottons. **Fabri's** specialises in shoes, but has other leather goods as well. **Kanguroo** has a great selection of clothes and accessories for children. There is also a furniture store, a computer shop, a medical centre, an ophthalmologist, a dentist and a veterinarian. **Mercadona** has lots of parking (some shaded) and is opposite **Mesón Son Caliu** (► 79), the best bargain lunch on the island.

Puerto Portals

Beautiful Puerto Portals (► 70) is basically a shopping centre by the sea. Most shops specialise in top-quality designs which come with hefty price tags. The Swedish-owned **Blue Marin** houses a collection of casual cottons from bikinis and chinos to chic striped shirts and backpacks. **Top As** sells shoes and accessories bearing such names as Mario Cerutti, Alberto Gozzi and Osualdo Martini. At the **Fashion House** you'll find Brooksfield, Moschino, Missoni and Versace labels. **Le Pirat**, which also has boutiques in Port d'Andratx, Peguera and Cala d'Or, stocks a fine array of elegant casuals. You can buy yourself a watch or jewellery bearing such names as Rolex, Bulgari or Chopard at Relojería Alemana, hidden in the corner beside the news kiosk. At **Ports**, who have branches in Port de Pollença and Peguera, you'll find the latest in yachting fashion and accessories, including Blue Willi's natural fabrics. Several yacht brokers are more than willing to sell you one of the big, gleaming beauties moored in the marina. If the up-market prices get you down, plan to be here in early April for the **Nautical Street Market** where bargains run from navigation instruments to fishing tackle and designer clothes: proceeds go to the Red Cross Sea Rescue.

Where to...
Be Entertained

Most major hotels provide some type of evening entertainment, and some arrange transport for evenings out. Ask at the reception desk about evening options.

Night-life

If you like night-life, you may like Magaluf, the hottest hub west of Palma. Try Lluna (Punta Ballena 12; beside the old Atlantic Hotel) with music from reggae to heavy heartbeat, or the BCM Disco Empire (Avinguda S'Olivera 13), the biggest night-spot on the island. At Casino Mallorca (tel: 971 130000; fax: 971 131465; www.casinodemallorca.com), just west of Magaluf, you can try your luck at roulette, black jack and

one-armed bandits. This is the only casino on the island. Non-gamblers might enjoy the art exhibit, the music in the Gato Negro bar, or the Las Vegas-style dinner and cabaret show in the Casino Paladium; if you skip the dinner and just enjoy a drink with the show, it's cheaper. Open Monday to Saturday 8 pm to 4 am; Sunday 3 pm to 4 am.

Outdoor Activities

The kind climate and the spectacular scenery are continually inviting you out of doors – for water sports at the beaches and bays, and for walking, hiking, cycling and horse-riding on the roads that crisscross the island. **Golf** Mallorca has 18 golf-courses, all with spectacular settings and modern amenities. In a valley of

small hills covered with pine, almond and oak trees, the challenging 18-hole Bendinat golf-course (tel: 971 405200) in Costa d'en Blanes is short and narrow (par 70). The 18-hole Poniente course (tel: 971 130148), just west of Magaluf, has a par of 72 and offers one-to-five-day coaching programmes for both beginners and experienced players. The Santa Ponça course (tel: 971 690211), several times the setting for the Balearic Open, has a demanding 18 holes (par 72). Long hitters will like the 10th hole (590m; par 5), one of the longest in Europe. The Son Vida (tel: 971 791210); also 18 holes and par 72, is a short course with lots of trees around the fairways and four lakes. The Son Vida Golf Club, one of the first on the island, set the standards in the 1960s, and golfers still love it.
Mini-golf If you don't take golf too seriously, head for Fantasia (tel: 971 135040) in Palma Nova. You can take your pick of three 18-hole courses, set among waterfalls, lakes,

streams and caves in a tropical garden with a cafeteria and terrace.
Sailing If you'd rather be at sea with the breezes, contact the Calanova Sailing School (tel: 971 402512), which offers a great variety of options for holiday sailing. Various regattas take place throughout the summer. If you'd prefer to be underwater, inquire about scuba-diving excursions and instruction at your hotel reception or at the local tourist office.
Water fun If your children are bored at the beach, take them to Aquapark (tel: 971 130811), Carretera Cala Figuera, Magaluf. They'll love the 10 million litres of water for kamikazes, soft slides, the adventure river and the swimming-pool. Parents can relax on the central oasis and listen to their children scream with pleasure as they whoosh down the slides. There is a miniature aquapark for very young children. If the kids ask what you're going to do for an encore, there's a go-karting track next door.

Tramuntana

Getting Your Bearings

Visible from all over Mallorca, the dramatic Tramuntana range is a wilderness of peaceful peaks and valleys – except when the fierce Tramuntana winter wind blows in from the north, or when the tour buses pile up in Valldemossa or in front of the Lluc Monastery.

The neo-classical Cartoixa church dates from the 18th century and has only a single nave

The range, averaging 10km in width, stretches from Sa Dragonera 90km north-east to Cape Formentor. In some places, steep barren cliffs and forests of Aleppo pine and holm oak plunge straight down to the sapphire sea. In the central part of the range are the highest peaks, several towering more than 1,000m skywards. The highest, Puig Major, rises 1,445m and is crowned with a communications complex reminiscent of two gargantuan white golf balls.

Page 83: The Nus de la Corbeta road winds down from the high Tramuntana to the north coast

Punta
Galera

Cap de
Catalunya

Es
Colomer

Cala Figuera

Cap de
Formentor

PM221

▲334m En Fumat

Formentor 9

Cala Sant
Vicenç

Formentor

Cala Murta

Platja de
Formentor

Punta de
l'Avançada

Port de
Pollença

Badia de
Pollença

Pollença

▲320m
Puig Maria

PM220

| 0 | | 5 km |
| 0 | . | 5 miles |

Port de Sóller's increasingly popular seafront is being developed into an attractive promenade

This scenic drive across the Tramuntana mountain range takes in beaches, a boat trip and a choir concert at Lluc Monastery.

Tramuntana in Two Days

Day 1

Morning

Make an early start in Valldemossa (➤ 88), giving yourself time to explore La Cartoixa (only one of the two towers has a cupola, left) and take in a Chopin piano recital in King Sancho's Palace. After coffee at Bar Meriendas (➤ 105), take the coast road to Deià (➤ 91) and climb the steep streets of the village to see Robert Graves's simple tombstone in the churchyard on top of the hill. The road continues through the hamlet of Lluch-Alcari, with views down over the coast, then drops to the Sóller Valley (➤ 93). In Sóller, head for a *tapas* lunch in the main square, Plaça Constitució, where the bars serve freshly squeezed orange juice from oranges grown in the valley.

Afternoon

Hop on the Orange Express tram to Port de Sóller for an afternoon on the beach. Alternatively, get there in time to catch the last boat (3 pm in summer, pictured below) to Sa Calobra (➤ 103), a much easier way to approach this beauty spot than on the challenging drive.

Evening

Sóller (main plaza pictured left) and Port de Sóller are much quieter once the day-trippers have gone home. Choose one of the fish restaurants by the harbour to enjoy a relaxing meal, then work off your dinner with a stroll around the bay.

Day 2

Morning

The highest section of the Tramuntana is between Sóller and Lluc, and you need to concentrate on your driving as the road winds through tunnels, gorges and mountain passes. Pause for a cool drink at Mirador Ses Barques (➤ 105) to admire the view over Port de Sóller and steel yourself for the drive ahead. The road passes two reservoirs in the shadow of Puig Major, Mallorca's highest mountain, on its way to Lluc (its coronated Virgin is pictured right, ➤ 96). Try to arrive by 11 am to catch the concert by Els Blavets, then walk up the Way of the Rosary for views over the valleys before lunch in the old monks' refectory, Sa Fonda (➤ 106).

Afternoon

The journey across the mountains ends on the Formentor peninsula (➤ 99), with an hour or two on Formentor beach (above) followed by the drive out to the lighthouse at dusk.

Valldemossa

This mossy vale is one of the loveliest areas on the island, but its exceptional beauty and proximity to Palma (17km) have made Valldemossa so popular that droves of tour buses have faded some of its glory. The best approach is from Palma, where as you drive through a narrow mountain pass, the tiled green belfry of La Cartoixa and the huddle of earth-coloured homes with their manicured terrace gardens come into view. This is Mallorca's highest town at 437m.

SANTA CATALINA THOMAS PREGAU PER NOSALTRES

It was near Valldemossa at Miramar that Ramón Llull set up a foreign-language school seven centuries ago; Llull would probably be excited to hear all the languages spoken here now, but when tourists return to their hotels at sundown, Mallorquín takes over until sunrise. Archduke Luis Salvador who subsequently owned Miramar had a statue of Llull placed here.

Highlights

• Mallorca's only saint, **Santa Catalina Thomás**, was born in Valldemossa in 1531. The peasant girl became a nun and spent most of her exemplary life of 43 years in Palma's Santa Magdalena convent where, it is said, she mixed sand with her soup to help avoid the cardinal sin of gluttony. Most Valldemossa homes display a colourful tile picture near the front door asking the saint for her blessing and local souvenir shops sell a variety of such tiles. Just north of Sant Bartomeu parish church, a five-minute walk from the town centre, the house where the saint was born (Carrer Rectoria 5) has been restored as a shrine. A statue of her stands beside a fountain outside the church.

Santa Catalina was canonised in 1627 and remains a revered presence in Valldemossa. Opposite: Valldemossa is likely to get a dusting of snow every decade

• George Sand was no saint but she made the town famous and also **La Cartoixa** the second most visited site on the island (after Palma's cathedral) through her book *A Winter in Majorca*, a sometimes brilliant, sometimes tedious account of a few months spent here with composer Frédéric Chopin during the winter of 1838–9. Along with Sand's two children, they

La Cartoixa	Costa Nord
✚ 179 D3	✚ 179 D3
✉ Plaça Cartoixa	✉ Avinguda Palma 6
☎ 971 612106	☎ 971 612425; www.costanord.com
⏰ Mon–Sat 9:30–6, 10–1, Mar–Oct; Mon–Sat 9:30–4:30, rest of year	⏰ Tue–Sun 10–8, in summer; 10–6, in winter
⛟ Moderate	⛟ Expensive

lived in a suite with beautiful gardens in the Carthusian monastery, shortly after the monks' cells had been converted to guest accommodation. The suite displays portraits, manuscripts and musical scores of the mismatched couple, along with Chopin's piano.

• The **Municipal Museum**, also within La Cartoixa, houses interesting books and paintings belonging to Archduke Luis Salvador, including the manuscript of his encyclopaedic nine-volume *Die Balearen*. Another room features an old printing press, a reminder that Nicolau Calafat established one here in the 15th century, only three years after Gutenberg produced his. Also in La Cartoixa is the neo-classical church with a dome decorated by frescoes painted by Fray Manuel Bayeu, brother-in-law of celebrated Spanish artist Francisco Goya. Upstairs, a display of modern art features works of such notables as Joan Miró, Picasso, Henry Moore, Max Ernst and Juli Ramis.

Chopin composed several nocturnes and the Raindrop Prelude in Mallorca

• The 17th-century **monks' pharmacy,** which served the town into the 20th century, is lined with painted wooden boxes, white ceramic jars trimmed with blue, and antique glass bottles, some still guarding potions from ages past. The small souvenir shop next door has some of the best prices in town.

• Next door to La Cartoixa is **King Sancho's Palace**, originally built as a hunting lodge in 1311, but rebuilt in the 16th century. The palace is sumptuously furnished with antiques, *objets d'art* and religious treasures, and the entry courtyard filled with rose-mary is quite endearing. A small concert hall inside the palace is the setting for piano concerts featuring Chopin classics. The palace can be visited on the same ticket as La Cartoixa.

• The American actor Michael Douglas has bought one of Archduke Luis Salvador's estates near Valldemossa and used his wealth and influence to promote the landscape and culture of the Tramuntana region. His new **Costa Nord Cultural Centre** opened in 2000 and features a film in which Michael Douglas describes his passion for this part of Mallorca.

TAKING A BREAK

The Bar Meriendas (➤ 105) is a popular spot, probably thanks to the bags of oranges hanging outside. Try the light sugar-dusted *cocas de patatas* (potato buns), a local speciality along with the thick hot chocolate. The coffee is very good too.

VALLDEMOSSA: INSIDE INFO

Top tips Most of Valldemossa's many visitors arrive by tour bus by day, so at night it's a different town. Can Mario, close to La Cartoixa, serves good Mallorcan-style meals and has a few spartan rooms for overnight guests (➤ 106).

• Prices at the souvenir stands throughout La Cartoixa are often lower than at the souvenir shops on the pedestrian routes from the car-parks to La Cartoixa.

Deià

Deià is one of those places that is too pretty for its own good. This village of honey-stone houses in the shadow of the Teix Mountain has become a magnet for wealthy foreigners, and few local people can afford a home here. Perhaps fortunately, there is nowhere for tour buses to park in the village, but that hasn't kept visitors away or dozens of artists from settling happily here, even though the light of day is limited by the powerful peak.

Writers and Artists

Foreign writers found the valley before foreign artists. American author Gertrude Stein advised British *confrère* Robert Graves to head here in the late 1920s. "It's a paradise," she said, "if you can stand it." He did, and lived in Deià most of the rest of his life. He loved the village, its people and the landscapes. Here he found muses to inspire not only his *chef d'œuvre The White Goddess*, but also the renowned *I, Claudius*. He is buried in the graveyard outside the church with its square tower crowning the village. The many expatriates who have lived here over the years have hardly changed the character of the village. Unbothered by outsiders, locals maintain traditions and celebrate age-old fiestas much as they always have.

Deià remains one of the most charming villages in Spain

DAMARC ✚ 179 D3 ✉ Carrer Es Clot, s/n ☎ 971 639001 🕐 Tue–Sun 10:30–1, in summer 💰 Donation

Although several shops sell the work of local artists and artisans, the best place to see their collective work is on the northern outskirts of town at Hotel La Residencia (► 104). The hotel, built from two 16th-century manor houses, is decorated with local art and recently opened an exhibit area for local artists.

At the Deià Archaelogical Museum and Research Centre (DAMARC) in the town centre, you can see remnants of the work of earlier artists, much earlier – for example, Jurassic. The museum showcases pottery, jewellery, tools and bones unearthed in the area, which indicate that people were living here at least 7,000 years ago.

TAKING A BREAK

The absolutely best place to take a break is the outdoor terrace overlooking the village at La Residencia (► 104).

The south-facing terrace at Hotel La Residencia is a peaceful spot to admire the view

---

DEIÀ: INSIDE INFO

Top tip It's a half-hour hike down to Deià beach. Head down the road towards Sóller and turn left at the sign pointing to the Depuradora. After the wooden ravine, you arrive at a lovely rocky cove with deep clear water, great for swimming and snorkelling. A beach bar and restaurant serve refreshments in summer.

Sóller Valley

Prosperous, shady Sóller is one of Mallorca's most pleasing small towns, set in a fertile valley of citrus groves between the mountains and the sea. The novelist D H Lawrence said that he felt like a bumblebee here among all the orange, lemon and grapefruit plantations. These days, throughout the summer, Sóller is crawling with tourists, who arrive for the day on the vintage train from Palma and take the tram down to the port.

Until the railway from Palma arrived in Sóller in 1912, the link with the rest of the island was limited to the mule track over the pass. That track became a road but it had hairpin bends that only a Formula 1 racing driver would enjoy driving. Consequently, Sóller looked north to Barcelona and Marseilles, but in 1997, the 3-km long Sóller Tunnel (toll) through the Coll de Sóller opened, and this once isolated valley became much closer to the rest of Mallorca.

Sóller

Arriving at the railway station, walk down the hill to the main square, Plaça Constitució. On the south side stands Sant Bartomeu Church with its beautiful rose window and modernist façade designed by Catalan architect and

---

Natural Science Museum
- ✚ 179 E4
- ✉ Carretera Palma–Port de Sóller, Km 30
- ☎ 971 634064
- 🕐 Tue–Sat 10–6, Sun 10–2
- 💶 Moderate

Riding the Rails

The first railway in Mallorca started running in 1875, between Palma and Inca, but service on the 27-km track between Palma and Sóller began only in 1912. The rustic old iron horse provides a continuing collage of magnificent mountain scenes and rumbles through a dozen tunnels. The train takes an hour to travel between Palma and Sóller, and runs five or six times daily from 8 am until 8 pm (tel: 971 630130 for the timetable). The mid-morning tourist train stops for 10 minutes at the Mirador del Pujol den Banya for a view of Sóller and photo opportunities.

The Orange Express Tram connecting Sóller with Port de Sóller, a 30-minute trip, runs every half-hour in summer and every hour in winter. The windows open on the old wagons, giving a clear view of homes and gardens along the way. The tram stops often along the 5-km route, but you can ask to hop off anywhere.

Gaudí disciple Joan Rubió, who also designed the bank building next door. You might want to sit in the shade of a plane tree at any of several cafés in the plaza and try a fresh orange juice. Sóller oranges enjoy the reputation of being the best on the island; they're of old stock, smaller and more acidic. Sóllerics also love home-made ice-cream, and the shop on the north side of the plaza sells up to 30 flavours, depending on the fruits in season. If you sit long enough in the plaza, you will see the tram to Port de Sóller as it rattles past. You might want to stroll east from the plaza along Carrer Sa Lluna (Moon Street) with its numerous shops and old mansions built by emigrants who had returned from France, where they went to live when the orange groves suffered a blight in the 1860s. Number 50 Casa de la Lluna, which has an intriguing relief of a Buddha-like face in a crescent moon, gives its name to the street.

Above: Sant Bartomeu Church looms over the main plaza in Sóller

Previous page: The Orange Express tram runs along the beach at Port de Sóller

• On the edge of town on the Palma–Port de Sóller road, a big stone talaiot (a reproduction of a historic watch-tower) marks the Museu Balear de Ciències Naturals. While the elegant *fin de siècle* merchant manor houses a limited but interesting fossil collection and an impressive looking research library, the real treasure is the botanic garden at the back. Here grow 400 species of flora from the Balearics, the Canary Islands and other parts of the world. One area is devoted to succulents, another to herbs and spices, and another to various citrus and other trees. The Jardí Botànic is proud of its seed bank, which should ensure the conservation of native plants well into the next century.

Ses Valentes Dones

One of Sóller's liveliest fiestas is Ses Valentes Dones (the Valiant Women), held every May in honour of the battle in 1561 when African pirates attacked. Sóllerics Francesca and Catalina successfully fought them off with clubs made from mulberry wood and became heroines forever. As well as the celebration itself, the competition among local women for the leading roles in the battle re-enactment every year is exciting.

Port de Sóller

Part fishing village, part military base, part holiday resort, Port de Sóller is a natural harbour set inside a perfect fish-shaped bay. In summer it is hard to move here for the crowds of day-trippers arriving by tram. By the time you get there, the waterfront will have been turned into a

Opposite: The dramatic view from the terrace at Ses Barques

pedestrian promenade. The beach is close to the town centre so is not pristine and the bay's narrow mouth slows the circulation of sea water. The last tram stop is at the marina and from here, *golondrinas* (excursion boats) flit along the coast north to Cala Tuent, Sa Calobra, El Torrent de Pareis and south to Sa Dragonera. On the hill above the port is the oldest part of the town. Es Port, once a medieval manor, is now a gracious and elegant inn.

It's a pleasant hour's walk, paved all the way, around the bay and along the beach and up to the lighthouse, Faro de Punta Grossa. The views of the coast are spectacular, especially at sunset. The lighthouse immediately above the marina is part of a military base and not accessible to the general public.

TAKING A BREAK

For good seafood, try Sa Llotja des Peix on the fishing dock or El Pirata on a narrow side street running up from the port.

Port de Sóller boat excursions
✚ 179 D4
☎ 971 633109
🕐 To Sa Calobra: three times daily in summer, 11:30 am daily in winter. Other destinations in summer only.

SÓLLER VALLEY: INSIDE INFO

Top tip If you're travelling by car and want to take the train to Sóller, catch it in Bunyola instead of Palma. The best scenery is between Bunyola and Sóller, it's easier to park and you avoid the traffic congestion of Palma.

• There are several good walks in this area, including a coastal path to Deià and an old mule track from Sóller to the port. Shops in Port de Sóller sell walking maps and several local guides offer excursions.

Lluc

This high Shangri-la-like valley surrounded by sierras is both the spiritual soul of the island and a popular outdoor excursion and ecological centre. Mallorcans also often drive up the winding roads on Sundays simply to lunch in one of several rustic restaurants serving wild game.

Prehistoric islanders probably worshipped at a Talaiotic temple here at the time when the Romans arrived on Mallorcan shores two millennia ago. A nearby cave houses a prehistoric burial chamber dating from the 4th century BC. The current church, however, has its origins in a 13th-century legend (▶ panel). Old parchments record that pilgrims were progressing to Santa Maria de Lluc as early as 1273. Now every August, some 30,000 Mallorcans set off from Palma to walk the 48km across the plains and up the mountains to the monastery in one night.

The Ave Maria basilica dome combines fine art with stunning architecture

El Santuari de Lluc (Lluc Monastery) dates from the Middle Ages, and the present basilica was built in the 17th century. The most interesting elements of the complex are

Wandering Statue

According to legend, a young shepherd boy named Lluch (Lucas) found a stone statue of the dark-skinned Virgin in the forest seven centuries ago and took it to a local priest in nearby Escorca. Three times the priest put the Virgin in his church and three times she reappeared back in the forest. So the priest ordered a chapel to be built to house the restless rock sculpture, now La Moreneta, the Virgin of Lluc.

El Santuari de Lluc
✚ 179 F4 ☎ 971 871525; fax: 971 517096; www.lluc.net

Museum
🕐 Daily 10–1, 2:30–5:15
💶 Inexpensive

If you miss Els Blavets chorale singing morning mass, listen to their rehearsal later in the day

Olives

Mallorcan tables present dozens of different olives – bitter little green ones pickled with fennel, big round green olives stuffed with anchovies, brown olives marinated with garlic and the firm black ones often associated with Greece. The colour depends on the time of harvesting: the longer they stay on the tree, the darker they become.

Long regarded as a healthy food, olives are rich in fibre and vitamin E. The fruit juice, olive oil, sometimes called green gold, varies from golden to dark green in colour. Olive oil contains only beneficial fatty acids and has no cholesterol. The extra virgin, considered best because it has less than one per cent oleic acid, comes from the first of three pressings where no heat is used.

the cloister, the rich collection of art objects and religious imagery in the museum, and the venerated La Moreneta, a dark-skinned Virgin with the child Jesus in her left arm; he is holding the Book of Life with the signs alpha and omega on the open pages. The Virgin's ornate crown of jewels does not suit her simple face, but her serene and knowing smile makes her endearing.

Another highlight of any visit here is Els Blavets, the resident boys' choir, which has been a part of the Augustinian monastery since 1531. Dressed in white shirts and blue soutanes, they sing in the basilica at the morning mass and evening vespers. The rest of the day they're busy rehearsing, studying their school work or playing soccer like Spanish boys everywhere. The boys take off the last weekend of every month and the entire month of July to go home to visit their families.

Bishop Campins promoted Lluc early in the 20th century

The 20-minute trek along the broad path up the rocky hill behind the monastery leads to a tall cross brought here in 1910 by pilgrims from Jerusalem. Sculptures by Antoni Gaudí and Joan Rubió illustrate the mysteries of the rosary along the way. More breathtaking are the splendid views of the surrounding orchards and pastures rimmed by grey rock and green forest.

At the monastery restaurant and several others in the area, both food and service are excellent. You're welcome to rent a room in the ancient pilgrims' quarters (➤ 104) to stay the night. In front of the monastery on Pilgrims' Plaza, there's a café/bakery, a monks' herbal pharmacy, and a glass-sided shop selling olive oil, embroideries, almond blossom perfume and other souvenirs.

TAKING A BREAK

Not far from Lluc at Escorca try Es Guix (tel: 971 517092), a lovely terrace restaurant with a swimming-pool to enjoy.

LLUC: INSIDE INFO

Top tip You can collect water from the mountain spring if you bring your own bottles. Go through the car-park at Lluc and then turn left. Within a few metres you will see black wrought-iron gates on your right. At the end of a stone path between two rock walls is a public fountain (with a spigot) of mountain spring water. Sometimes there is a queue of islanders, but there are stone benches for waiting and, when it is your turn, you can take as much drinking water as you want.

• The choirboys sing twice a day but the tour groups all come to the morning performance at 11:15. For a more peaceful and spiritual experience, stay till dusk or stay overnight and go to the service of vespers at 7:30 instead.

Formentor

The hair-raising drive across this wild and rugged peninsula is probably the most scenic in Mallorca, as tall cliffs give way to hidden coves where the Tramuntana drop down into the sea.

The road begins in Port de Pollença. Concentrate hard and keep your eyes on the road as it climbs to the *mirador* at Es Colomer. From here it descends in twists and turns and opens up to a crescent of pale sandy beach stretching 1km along the crystal sea. The beach is popular for coach day trips, for families looking for a safe clean beach, and for swinging singles just chilling out. Active options include windsurfing and water-skiing. Sleek yachts anchored offshore may belong to superstars, old aristocracy or *nouveaux riches* staying at the Hotel Formentor.

Flora
Honeysuckle, heather and lavender like to grow near the many wild olive trees. There are countless groves of pine and holm oak, and centennial elms reminiscent of the huge dark elm that Virgil and Sybil found growing at the gateway to Hell. The round red fruit on the strawberry tree, from the Arbutus family, is quite tasty. One of the prettiest wild flowering plants is the cyclamen. Nine species of orchid and 13 species of fern grow alongside mountain streams.

The fishing is good in the northern waters of the Formentor peninsula

✚ 180 C5

Fauna

About the only wildlife left in the Tramuntana are birds, rabbits and wild goats. There are several colonies of Eleonora's falcon, ospreys, gulls, cormorants and petrels. Eagles, hawks, kites and kestrels fly all along the mountain range. The most spectacular bird, the black vulture with a 3-m wingspan, is rarely seen elsewhere in the world. There are also barn owls, scops owls, alpine owls and white-throated owls.
If you're hiking down a secluded mountain trail, you may come across the Mallorcan midwife frog, the ferreret (➤ 30).

In the late 1920s and 1930s, Formentor was made famous by celebrities and the wealthy visiting the luxurious hotel, built by Argentinian couple Adan Diehl and Mercedes Popolitzio. Streamlined motorcruisers and tall-masted yachts continue to come and go, reminiscent of the times when the Prince of Wales entertained Mrs Simpson on the Royal Yacht or when the Onassis family, the Rainiers of Monaco, John Wayne and Sir Winston Churchill made Formentor their playground.

From Formentor the road continues through the pine woods for another 10km to reach the silver-domed lighthouse on the edge of the cliffs. Shortly after passing a solitary pine, a steep track leads down to the isolated cove of Cala Figuera, an idyllic spot with crystalline blue-green water for swimming. The road now passes through a tunnel on its way to the lighthouse, where parking can be a problem in summer. There is a small café and wonderful views from the terrace, stretching all the way to Menorca on a clear day.

TAKING A BREAK

In summer, it's advisable to pack a picnic, since the beach bar and café is often very busy. Or you might enjoy an elegant lunch on the tranquil terrace of the Hotel Formentor. The terrace looks over the lush gardens of the hotel and out to the bay.

FORMENTOR: INSIDE INFO

Top tip If you're driving to Formentor, consider going in the early morning or late afternoon when it's not so crowded. If you're just going to enjoy the seaside, you can travel by *golondrina* (boat) from the dock in Port de Pollença. It's a pleasant 30-minute journey each way. Away from the dock where boats disembark, the beach is less crowded.

Hidden gems It's a picturesque 2-km walk from the road between Formentor and the lighthouse into nearby Cala Murta, a small deep-water cove that is ideal for swimming and snorkelling. A yacht or two may drop anchor in the little bay. The restaurant here is open in summer.

In more depth The mirador at Es Colomer, 6km from Port de Pollença, features a 300-m long walkway looking straight down 200m to the sea. In the background is the rock islet of Es Colomer (the dovecote), named for the wild doves that shelter here along with the seagulls. Across the road is an old watch-tower. The reward for the half-hour hike up to it is a panorama of the peninsula. When sunrise or sunset rinse with gold the surrounding sea and mountains, the grandeur is breathtaking.

At Your Leisure

🔢 Son Marroig

This magnificent estate, now a museum and shrine to Austrian aristocrat, scholar and ecologist Archduke Luis Salvador, was once his favourite home. Parts of the ground floor and the first floor are open to the public.

On view are many photos and drawings of the Archduke (with his inseparable parasol), along with some of his notes and sketches. There is also a collection of old Mallorcan furniture, Hispanic-Arabic ceramics, and paintings by Antonio Ribas Prats whose family inherited the estate when the Archduke died from elephantitis in Bohemia in 1915.

The house, hovering 300m above the craggy coast, has a defence tower built to watch for pirates in the 16th century. The tower was not 100 per cent successful: in one of his books, the Archduke tells the story of a woman from Sóller who was kidnapped by pirates from this tower and never heard from again.

The beautiful romantic garden behind the mansion runs out to a neo-classical columned rotunda, built from white carrara marble imported from Italy. The lookout offers a spectacular view of Sa Foradada (➤ 162), a rocky peninsula jutting out to sea.

Son Marroig was home to Archduke Luis Salvador who fell in love with it at first sight

➕ 179 D4
✉ Valldemossa–Deià road (C-710)
☎ 971 639158
🕐 Mon–Sat 9:30–2, 3–7:30 (5:30 in winter) 💷 Inexpensive

The Archduke, born in Tuscany where his father was king, wandered the Mediterranean aboard his yacht *Nixe* and arrived in Mallorca in 1867. He bought Son Marroig a few years later. The Archduke spoke 14 languages and developed an encyclopaedic knowledge of botany. Famous for his hospitality, he offered three days of food and lodging to anyone needing a place to stay; unlike Chopin and George Sand, the Archduke was loved by the Mallorcans. One of his passions was horse-riding; he built bridle paths throughout his estates, and these have become mountain trails that hikers follow today.

5 Alfàbia

With their lily ponds, bamboo groves and soaring palms, the classical gardens at Alfàbia are one of the few legacies of Islamic rule in Mallorca. They make a peaceful place to spend a couple of hours, strolling along covered walkways and sitting in the shade of orange trees listening to the sound of water from the spray pergola. The gardens are situated on the south side of the Coll de Sóller, near the entrance to the Sóller tunnel. The restaurant in the car-park, Ses Porxeres, specialises in Catalan game dishes.

🕂 179 D3
✉ Carretera Palma–Sóller, Km 14
☎ 971 613123
🕐 Mon–Fri 9:30–6:30, Sat 9:30–1, Apr–Sep; Mon–Fri 9:30–5:30, Sat 9:30–1, rest of year
💶 Moderate

6 Fornalutx

Fornalutx is one of the prettiest mountain villages on the island, or was, until the word got out. The place is often crowded with cars and bus tours for much of the day in high season, but the crowds leave in the evening. If you can find a parking place, stroll through the narrow cobbled streets to the tiny main square. About half the beautiful old ochre stone homes here belong to foreigners. The federal government has declared the village a cultural monument, so strict building codes are now in place.

If it's too crowded, have a bite to eat or a coffee on a restaurant terrace overlooking the village. The view across the broad valley of the thousands of orange trees to Puig Major, combined with the soft scent of

Tir amb passeta

It was probably in the ancient village of Fornalutx that the Talaiotic sport of *tir amb passeta* began. Using a strong sling, and a stone as the ball, skilled slingers could knock down a bird in flight 100m away. The story goes that young boys were not allowed to eat dinner until they had felled a bird in flight, so were encouraged to hone their skills. When the Romans arrived on the island, they hired these local hunters as mercenaries in their armies. The name "Balearics" comes from the Greek word *ballein* – to throw from a sling.

The name Fornalutx comes from the Mallorcan words for oven and light

A rock arch at Sa Calobra frames splendid seascapes

orange blossoms wafting up from the orchards below, is paradise enough for one day.

🞥 179 E4

✉ 5km northeast of Sóller (via Biniaraix)

7 Sa Calobra

This tourist honeypot has long been discovered by the masses and though it remains an undeniably beautiful spot the effect is somewhat spoilt by the proliferation of tour buses and souvenir shops. You can get here by boat from Port de Sóller, but for a truly memorable experience take the road which snakes down from the Tramuntana. There is curve after curve for 12km, and with every bend comes another spectacular view, until you almost reach the sea at a grove of 100-year-old olive trees. There is limited parking down here, so abandon your vehicle wherever you can find a parking spot and continue on foot. The blue Mediterranean is straight ahead. Continue along to the right for about 10 minutes, and the mouth of the Torrent de Pareis will open before you. This awesome chasm, a dry river bed in summer, has been forged by winter rains thundering from the mountains a distance of 15km to the sea. The torrent drops some 600m on its relentless course, carving dizzying cliffsides and a creek bed with boulders as big as bungalows. Here, just 35km from packed Arenal Beach in the south, is some of Spain's most rugged terrain. If you're fit and adventurous, you might want to come back another day and hike the 7km from Lluc down the chasm to the sea. In one place where the canyon narrows to 30m, the walls are 300m high; while you won't suffer from the sun, this pass is treacherous because flash floods caused by quick heavy rains can sweep hikers away. Be sure to go with a guide: every year a careless hiker doesn't make it and has to be carried out – not always alive.

Due to its isolation in the old days when the road down was merely a mule track, Sa Calobra used to be a refuge for pirates: on one occasion the buccaneer Redbeard kidnapped a local landowner nicknamed Calobra. As late as the mid-20th century, smugglers frequently received goods in these remote coves. Today tourism is more profitable.

If you want to stop here for lunch, there are several restaurants, but they generally follow that age-old maxim: the better the view, the worse the food. In summer when Sa Calobra is crowded with tourists, pack a picnic and enjoy it on the beach.

🞥 179 E5

Where to... Stay

Prices

Prices are for the least expensive double room in high season, IVA sales tax included. Prices may drop by up to 50 per cent in low season. Breakfast is usually included in the room price. € = under 60 Euros €€ = 60–120 Euros €€€ = over 120 Euros

Apartamentos El Encinar €€

On a steep cliff of oak and pine forest overlooking the sea in this region Archduke Luis Salvador loved, these modern furnished flats provide a great base for hiking the Tramuntana or for simply seeing Mallorca in general. The aparthotel has a swimming-pool, tennis-court, bar/restaurant and a children's playground. Minimum stay is one week.

🔢 179 D3 ✉ Carretera Valldemossa –Deià ☎ 971 612000; fax: 971 616019

Formentor Hotel €€€

This peninsular landmark has been an idyllic hideaway for the rich and famous since it was built in 1929. It sits in a forest of aleppo pine and has a remarkable view looking south over a crescent bay. The Formentor has all the superior facilities and service expected from a grand hotel (and a small cinema as well), yet its greatest appeal is probably in its terraces, gardens and solitary setting 300m above a sandy beach and crystal water. It's a short but challenging drive over the mountain pass to Port de Pollença.

🔢 180 C5 ✉ Formentor ☎ 971 899100; fax: 971 865155; email: reservas@hotelformentor.net; www.hotelformentor.net

Hotel Marina €

This basic little hotel overlooks the promenade and the bay; ask for a room with sea view and balcony. Staff are friendly and helpful. From here, you can easily walk to anywhere in the port; the tram from Sóller stops near by.

🔢 179 D4 ✉ Paseo de la Platja, Port de Sóller ☎ 971 631461; fax: 971 634182; email: info@hotelmarinasoller.com; www.hotelmarinasoller.com

La Residencia €€€

This luxury country house hotel, sold in 2002 by British entrepreneur Sir Richard Branson to the Orient Express hotel group, started the trend towards up-market rural tourism in Mallorca when it opened in 1984. Film stars, fashion models and European royalty have all stayed in this celebrity hideaway, converted from a pair of 16th and 17th-century fincas (manor houses) surrounded by orange groves. La Residencia has consistently been voted one of the top hotels in Europe. It has all the comforts you would expect, including both indoor and outdoor pools, and extras such as fresh fruit and flowers in the rooms. In winter the hotel organises activity breaks featuring painting, tennis, golf and beauty treatments. Tea on the terrace is a delightful treat in summer, while El Olivo restaurant (▶ 106), housed in the old Son Moragues olive press, offers elegance and fine dining. A great place for a romantic retreat.

🔢 179 D3 ✉ Finca Son Canals, Deià ☎ 971 639011; fax: 971 639370; email: reservas@hotel-laresidencia.com; www.hotel-laresidencia.com

Santuari de Lluc €

Although the hill town of Lluc bustles with visitors all day, it's marvellously peaceful at night. Rooms at the monastery, some with private bath, are clean and spartan. But here your window frames million-dollar views of the surrounding Lluc Valley. Although overnight rooms were originally meant for religious pilgrims, these days anyone is welcome.

🕇 179 F4 ⊠ Lluc, Escorca
☎ 971 871525; fax: 971 517096

Vistamar €€€

The Vistamar sits in a tranquil 100-ha estate of pines, oaks and ancient olives. The renovated Mallorcan mansion retains its original character and is lavishly furnished with antiques and complemented with fine 19th-century Spanish paintings. Amenities include telephones, satellite TV, mini-bars and a swimming-pool. The elegant restaurant and terrace, where you can dine in the shade of 400-year-old Greek cypress trees, specialises in Mediterranean cuisine and has an extensive wine cellar. A steep walking trail leads down 5km to Valldemossa beach.

🕇 179 D3 ⊠ Carretera Valldemossa–Andratx, Km 2
☎ 971 612300; fax: 971 612583; email: info@vistamarhotel.es; www.vistamarhotel.es

Where to...
Eat and Drink

Prices

The € amount indicates what you can expect to pay for a meal per person, excluding drinks, tax and tip. € = under 15 Euros   €€ = 15–30 Euros   €€€ = over 30 Euros

Bar Meriendas €

This is perhaps the most popular café in town, perhaps because of the seductive sacks of oranges hanging on the tree outside, or perhaps because of the beautiful marble table tops. Locals like their coffee and small, rich lamb pastries at the bar in front. Round fluffy potato buns dusted in icing-sugar and thick hot chocolate are specialities, but the fresh orange juice, coffee and other pastries are also good. Service is sometimes slow, so relax and enjoy the atmosphere.

🕇 179 D3 ⊠ Carrer Blanquera,
Valldemossa ☎ 971 616192
🕘 7 am until the last person leaves

Bens d'Avall €€€

Overlooking the romantic and dramatic north coast, this restaurant rates among the best on the island when you total up service, food, drink and the sunset from the terrace. But you don't want to drive these mountain roads after dark, and after a lot of food and drink, so you may miss dining under star-studded skies. Daytime views are equally dramatic, but visit when the weather is perfect because it's a shame to sit anywhere except on the terrace. The lobstser canneloni with parmesan and almonds is delectable and the creamy lemon pie irresistible.

🕇 179 D4 ⊠ Carretera Sóller–Deià, Km 56 (then a 2-km drive north) ☎ 971 632381 🕘 Tue–Sat 1–4, 8–11, in summer

Faro €€

Located above the fishing docks, the Faro features fresh fish and seafood. Ask about the catch of the day, for what the fishermen have caught that morning usually makes the best meal. Be sure to request a table with a view.

🕇 179 D4 ⊠ Cap Gros de Maleta, Port de Sóller ☎ 971 633752
🕘 Daily 12:30–3:30, 7:30–10:30

Mirador Ses Barques €€

Some people come for the panorama, some for the pan. The view over the north coast to Sóller, especially towards sunset when there is a golden glow to the mountains and sea, is breathtaking. Such local specialities as pork loin with cabbage or rabbit with onions are simply wonderful. Service is unpretentious and friendly. You can dine inside in the old-fashioned dining-room with the wrap-around view or upstairs on the terrace.

🕂 179 E4 ⊠ Carretera Sóller–Lluc, Km 45 ☎ 971 630792 ⏱ Tue–Sun 12:30–4; also Fri–Sat 7–10 pm

Can Mario €

There's no point in spending a fortune if a midday meal when you can feast in this modest *hostal* restaurant, one flight up, with a view overlooking the mountain pass to Palma. The women of the house, flushed from working in the hot kitchen, prepare and serve such home-style cooking as aubergines stuffed with ground pork and pork chops with fried potatoes.

🕂 179 D3 ⊠ Carrer Uetam 8, Valldemossa ☎ 971 612122 ⏱ Daily 1–3:30; also Fri–Sat 8:30–10:30 pm

Can Penasso €–€€

This 500-seat restaurant has been keeping Mallorcans and visitors contented with good food for 25 years, so there's little reason to stop now. Specialities include the traditional rice and meat dishes, tender lamb chops, grilled suckling pig and fried octopus. The restaurant is well known for its mousses, varying from apple to chocolate.

🕂 179 D3 ⊠ Carretera Palma–Sóller, Km 14.7, Bunyola ☎ 971 613261 ⏱ Thu–Tue 1–4, 8–12

El Olivo €€€

An elegant restaurant, this was once the Son Moragues olive mill (the press is still there), and is the only Deià restaurant with parking. Food and service are exceptionally fine. Try the creamy fish soup with herbs and prawn ravioli, and rack of lamb with cabbage and herbs in a mustard crust, then have coffee on the terrace looking out to Deià and Teix Mountain, the muse of Robert Graves. The wine cellar is

elaborate although some say wines are overpriced.

🕂 179 D3 ⊠ La Residencia Hotel, Deià ☎ 971 639392 ⏱ Daily 12:30–3:30, 7:30–11

Jaime €€

Jaime is a likely spot for the rich and famous to go when they want to eat in peace. The restaurant is run by Mallorcans who have spent decades in kitchens. The food is typically Mallorcan and tasty.

🕂 179 D3 ⊠ Carrer Arxiduc Lluis Salvador 13, Deià ☎ 971 639029 ⏱ Tue–Sun 12:30–3, 7:30–10:30

La Bodega €€

Owned by the company that owns the Taberna del Caracol (▶ 62) in Palma's old quarter, La Bodega is not quite up to par with its city cousin, but its scrambled eggs with prawns are famous. There is a sunny terrace for outdoor dining.

🕂 179 D3 ⊠ Carrer Arxiduc Lluis Salvador, 19, Deià ☎ 971 639139 ⏱ Tue–Sun 12:30–3:30, 7:30–11:30

Mirador Na Foradada €€

Located next door to Son Marroig, this restaurant features good Mallorcan cuisine and an awe-inspiring vista to the famous rock with the hole in it.

🕂 179 D3 ⊠ Carretera Valldemossa–Deià, Km 6 ☎ 971 639026 ⏱ Fri–Wed 12:30–3:30; also 7:30–10:30, Apr–Oct

Sa Cartoixa €–€€

This bustling Mallorcan restaurant in the centre of Valldemossa serves typical rustic fare such as roast shoulder of lamb, paella, *tumbet* (vegetable ratatouille) and a delectable almond tart. Alternatively you can just enjoy a *bocadillo* (sandwich) on the terrace in summer.

🕂 179 D3 ⊠ Plaça Ramón Llull 5, Valldemossa ☎ 971 612240 ⏱ Sun–Fri 8:30–6, in winter; 8:30 am–11 pm, in summer

Sa Fonda €€

Service is elegant and the setting divine, in this former refectory for monks. This restaurant maintains a monastic air, perhaps because of the wide stone arches which span the room. Specialities include rice with wild game, but the *pièce de résistance* is roast mountain kid with rosemary.

🔢 179 F4 ⌧ Luc Monastery ☎ 971 517022 ⏰ Wed–Mon 1–3.30, 7–9.30

Sebastian €€€

Set in an old town-house with bare stone walls, this elegant eatery specialises in Mediterranean food. The menu, while not extensive, presents such interesting options as fried mussels with artichoke hearts and tomatoes, lobster ravioli with green asparagus, and a platter of various Spanish cheeses which goes down very well with the home-made bread. Wines come from different regions of Spain and are reasonably priced. Staff are cordial and efficient.

🔢 179 D3 ⌧ Felipe Bauza, Deià ☎ 971 639417 ⏰ Thu–Tue 8 pm–11 pm, Feb–Nov

Where to... Shop

People don't usually come to the Tramuntana to shop, but that doesn't mean there's nothing to buy. Markets in Valldemossa (Sunday morning), and in Sóller and Bunyola (Saturday morning) offer the usual colourful array of clothes, crafts and foodstuffs.

Valldemossa

The route from the town car-parks to La Cartoixa is lined with stores selling ceramics and tiles, leather goods, cottons and silks, Swarovski crystal collectables, lacy shawls, T-shirts and other souvenirs.
Artesanías La Cartuja (Avinguda Palma 1) sells Mallorcan blown glass, silver thimbles, hand-painted enamelled earrings, and Lladró figurines by the dozens.

San Bruno (Carrer Marqués de Vivot 2) stocks a great selection of Santa Catalina tiles, yellow and blue ceramic ware, whimsical puppets and T-shirts. **Magdalena Alorda** (Avinguda Palma 5A) sells such crafts as olive-wood salad bowls, embroidered cottons and linens, blue coral and seashell jewellery, model ships and painted fans. **L'or de Mallorca** (Carrer Blanquerna 10–12), attractively decorated with rustic wine barrel rims from old bodegas, features blown glass in primary colours, and an exquisite array of gold and coral jewellery.

The bookshop on the corner of Plaça Cartoixa sells books, magazines and newspapers in Catalan, Spanish, English and German. The shops within La Cartoixa have a limited selection of goods but prices are generally lower.

Deià

If you've just won the lottery, you'll love the shop in **La Residencia Hotel** where you can find designer swimsuits from Israel, fine casual clothes from Italy, Yves Saint Laurent pens, handmade stationery, books, Majorica pearls and a small selection of other souvenirs. If you can't find anything you like here, **Casana** (opposite) has an exquisite array of jewellery made from gold and stainless steel inset with diamonds.

If your budget is limited, the **Herboristeria L'Arxiduc** (Carrer Arxiduc Lluís Salvador 2) next door offers an eclectic selection of home-made bread, medicinal herbs, natural cosmetics, clothes, books and flowers.

Sóller

The commercial centre of Sóller is Carrer La Lluna, but there are some good shops on other nearby streets. **Toni de Sa Coma** (Vicario Pastor 9) is a good antiques shop. The **Castaldo Paris shop** (Carrer Deià) sells earthenware casseroles, usable both on the hob and in the oven.

La Confianza (Carrer Lluna 7) sells an assortment of delicious pastries, but ensure you visit before you go to **Melissa** (Carrer Cristóbal Colón), because their exquisite selection of swimwear and lingerie may put you off pastries for a while. **Sa Fabrica de Gelats** (Plaça Mercat) offers an extensive selection of delicious ice-cream and sorbet flavours, many resulting from the valley's famous lemons, oranges and other fruits. **Fet a Sóller** (in the train station) sells quality work made by Sollerics with disabilities. Products vary from ceramics to marmalades and honeys to olive oil. The old olive-oil mill at nearby **Can Det**, one of the few still using hydraulic pressure to crush olives between two huge chunks of stone, produces only 10,000 litres a year, but any bottle you buy here will bring back memories of Mallorca for months to come. Olives used are from the same stock the Moors planted in the Tramuntana a millennium ago.

Where to...
Be Entertained

Here in these magical mountains, the entertainment is the outdoors, most of the time. But there are some cultural events, mostly in summer.

Cultural Events

Valldemossa The Costa Nord Cultural Centre (▶ 90) is home to Mediterranean Nights, a series of concerts featuring jazz and other musical tastes, from late June to late August. A number of leading international artists have performed here in recent years, including Van Morrison, flamenco guitarist Tomatito, and Cuban singer Compay Segundo. The renowned Chopin Festival (tel: 971 612351) takes place every July and August in La Cartoixa, although talented young

Mallorcan pianists play Chopin favourites every day all year in the concert hall in King Sanxo's Palace.
Deià Classical music concerts (tel: 971 639178) are held during July and August in the parish church, La Residencia and Son Marroig.
Port de Sóller The biggest fiesta of the year, early in May, commemorates a battle between the Moors and Christians 500 years ago.
Sóller The international festival of popular dances is held here in the last week of July every year.
Torrent de Pareis A choral concert is held on the beach in mid-July.
Lluc The Els Blavets Choir sings at morning mass and vespers in the church. The monastery gift shop sells cassettes and compact discs of these heavenly young voices.

Outdoor Activities

Boating Marina Sóller (Platja d'en Repic, Port de Sóller, tel: 971 634590) hires out sailing dinghies and motorboats, from 5m–18m long, for a half-day, a full day or a week. Barcos Azules (tel: 971 630170), also based in Port de Sóller, provides a catamaran service along the rugged coast from Sant Elm to Formentor.
Walking Walking, hiking and mountaineering are a way of life in the Tramuntana, a popular destination for European climbers. Bookshops in Sóller and at Lluc monastery sell guides and maps detailing both long and short walks in the area, and there are a number of local mountain guides offering accompanied walks. For serious hikers, the Ruta de la Pedra Seca (dry stone wall route) crosses the entire Tramuntana range from Andratx to Pollença.
Swimming Although most major hotels have swimming-pools, there are beaches at Valldemossa, Deià, Port de Sóller, Sa Calobra, Cala Sant Vicenç and Formentor.

East Coast

Getting Your Bearings

With long sandy beaches, gently sweeping bays and a trio of historic towns, the northeast corner of Mallorca has a wide and varied appeal. While the beach bums flock to the crowded resorts around Palma, this part of Mallorca appeals mainly to families seeking an active holiday, combining days on the beach with sightseeing, cycling and walking in the hills.

Cap de Catalunya
Cala Figuera
Cap de Formentor
Es Colomer
▲334m En Fumat
PM221
Cala Murta
Punta Galera
Cala Sant Vicenç
Coves de l'Alzinaret
2
Punta Beca
Formentor
Platja de Formentor
Punta de l'Avançada
Cap de Pinar
Port de Pollença
838m ▲ Ternelles
Pollença
1
C710
3
Badia de Pollença
Bonaire
Península de Alcúdia
Cap de Menorc
▲326m Puig Maria
Alcúdia
5
PM220
Alcúdia & Port d'Alc
Pollentia
4
Llac Gran
Port d'Alcúdia
La Gaviotas
Badia
C713
C712
Platja de Muro
d'Alcúdi

Resorts like Port d'Alcúdia and Cala Millor may pulsate to the disco beat, but, for the most part, the towns around this coastline are tastefully restrained in summer and almost totally deserted in winter, with few of the excesses that characterise resorts like Arenal and Magaluf. When you look at a map of Mallorca, it seems somehow appropriate that Pollença Bay looks out towards quiet, low-key Menorca while Palma faces brash, in-your-face Ibiza.

Parc Natural de S'Albufera
Can Picafort
Son Baulo
Sa Pobla
Co Sa
3
6 **Muro**
PM341
PM343
Santa Margalida
Ses Pastores

The Romans established their capital at Pollentia, on the site of present-day Alcúdia, which might be the island capital today but for an accident of history. When Jaume I set out to capture Mallorca from the Moors in 1229, he planned to land on the east coast in Pollença Bay. When a storm blew his ships off course, he landed in Palma instead, leaving Alcúdia as a small provincial town with Roman remains which are still being uncovered to this day.

Beside the beaches, the main attractions are found in the three towns of Alcúdia, Artà and Pollença. Each of these contains enough sights to keep anyone occupied for a day – particularly if you go on market day, when the towns burst into life and the streets are filled with stalls selling everything from vegetables to handmade pottery. When you want to get away from it all, take a walk in the S'Albufera wetlands (► 165), a paradise for bird-watchers with several footpaths and cycle trails.

Port de Pollença, its development carefully controlled, is one of the most up-market towns in Mallorca

Page 109: The Roman theatre in Alcúdia is the only one found on the island

★ Don't Miss

At Your Leisure

Visit the towns of Pollença, Alcúdia and Artà and still find time for an afternoon on the beach on a gentle tour of this region.

East Coast in Two Days

Day 1

Morning

Explore the streets and squares of Pollença (symbolised by a cockerel, right, ➤ 126). If you can, come on Sunday, when the cafés are full of chatter and the town is taken over by one of Mallorca's liveliest markets. Wander out to the Roman bridge (➤ 117), then climb the Calvary steps or make the trek up to Puig Maria (➤ 156) for views down over the town. Wind down with lunch at one of several excellent restaurants and cafés around the main square.

Afternoon

Spend a couple of hours soaking up the sun on one of the region's beaches (➤ 114). Serious sun-worshippers should head straight down to Port de Pollença and make for the less crowded southern end of the beach away from the marina. The more adventurous can take a bus from Pollença to Cala Sant Vicenç and hike back over the hills to Pollença Bay.

Evening

Enjoy a romantic stroll along the Pine Walk in Port de Pollença as the sun sets over the bay, then choose a seat under the fig tree at Balada del Agua del Mar (➤ 129) or any of the other beachside restaurants.

Day 2

Morning

Make an early start to explore the ruins of Roman Pollentia (➤ 117) before the tour groups start to arrive. Afterwards, take a walk around the walled town of Alcúdia (➤ 120) and have lunch at one of the cafés in Plaça Constitució.

Afternoon

Follow the coast road around Alcúdia Bay between the sand dunes and the S'Albufera reserve. If you feel like a break, park your car and clamber over the dunes on to the beach or follow one of the well-marked walking trails at S'Albufera (➤ 165). Continue to Artà (➤ 123) to visit the megalithic remains at Ses Païsses, then climb the steps to the sanctuary (relief detail right) above the town for views down over the roof-tops and out to sea.

Beaches

Everyone should be able to find a beach that suits them around this stretch of coast. The options range from Mallorca's longest beach at Alcúdia Bay, which is big enough to absorb seemingly endless crowds, to hideaways like Cala Mesquida and Colònia de Sant Pere, which though hardly undiscovered are a lot more peaceful.

Cala Sant Vicenç

This *cala* (cove) is actually on the north coast and has two coves with three small, perfect beaches, all within a stone's throw of cafés and souvenir shops, and all likely to be crowded from June to September. Rugged cliffs reach heavenwards to the east while rounded hills with hiking trails close in the *calas* from the west. But watch for the red flag in autumn, winter and spring because, when the winds pick up, the rolling surf can be dangerous. If you're here in winter, take time to watch the

waves roll in over the rocks: it's a hypnotic experience. The
northernmost *cala* has a gentle sloping beach, great for children
in the summertime. Lots of sea urchins, small octopus and fish
live among the rocks, so snorkelling is usually more interesting
here than on the east coast a few kilometres away.

Pollença Bay Beaches

The **Port de Pollença** beach, which curves around the north part
of the bay, is split in two by the marina. The narrow northern
beach, fringed by a flagstoned walkway shaded with pines,
widens into an elegant promenade lined with bars and cafés
where you can soak up sun and sangria and still see the kids on
the beach. South past the marina, the commercial zone fades and
the beach broadens for about a kilometre as it heads south
towards Alcúdia. For a lazy day, you can hire *chaises-longues* and
sun umbrellas. For aquatic action, there are sailing dinghies,
windsurfers, kayaks and pedaloes with water-slides, or you can
sign up for sailing or scuba lessons just offshore.

*Cala Barques is
the largest of
Cala Sant
Vicenç's coves*

Alcúdia Bay Beaches

Here is about 12km of broad sandy beach sloping gently out to
sea. The beachfront at Port d'Alcúdia is very built-up, but things

get quieter as you move around the bay. One of the
nicest sections is **Platja de Muro** because a few
kilometres have been declared a protected area,
and dunes with pine and tamarisk trees border the
fine white sand. Park at one of several areas indicated and hike over the dunes. If you're feeling
energetic, you can windsurf, water-ski, paraglide or
take a pedalo out into the bay. For an assortment
of bars, cafés and restaurants close by, choose
instead **Can Picafort** beach immediately south.

Beyond Can Picafort lies **Son Baulo**, where the
coast turns rocky, and the built-up area ends. Park
your vehicle near the Hotel Son Baulo and walk
south along the coastline (take care when the seas
are high!) about 20 minutes to the Son Real
Necropolis, a burial ground bordering the sea
dating from 700 BC. Archaeologists have found
evidence of trepanning, the medieval medical prac-
tice of bloodletting by piercing the skull with a
sharp stone, on several skulls discovered here. On
the small island just offshore, the remains of 230
people were found; sepulchres show rooms and
staircases, but water has eroded most of them away
over the millennia.

Colònia de Sant Pere

The Colònia de Sant Pere beach, a mere 130m in
length, is far enough off the beaten track to be
quite lovely, although it's hard to imagine this as
the king's hunting ground replete with wild boar as
it was 700 years ago. There is a small town, a yacht
club and a harbour that can be protected by sluice
gates from the east winds and seaweed. The rocky
shoreline is ideal for snorkelling.

Can Picafort resort is in the centre of the broad beach that curves around Alcúdia Bay

Cala Ratjada

This busy resort is popular with those who enjoy sailing, windsurfing, water-skiing and snorkelling. The largest beach is **Cala Agulla**, just north of Cala Ratjada; **Font de Sa Cala**, to the south, is livelier and has better water-sports facilities.

Cala Mesquida

This 600-m long stretch of sand and dunes, just north of Cala Ratjada, has been declared a protected area. All facilities are available. When a strong wind results in big rolling waves, surfers rush in from all over the island.

Cala Millor

If you're homesick for the concrete jungle, head to Cala Millor where 2km of sandy shore hold back the sea. All conveniences – hotels, apartments, shops and restaurants – line the shore. The neighbouring resort of **Cala Bona** is smaller and more intimate.

TAKING A BREAK

On Port de Pollença's Pine Walk the place for refreshment is Katy's (Passeig Vora Mar 65; tel: 971 866078) where the simple fare satisfies the heartiest appetite.

EAST COAST BEACHES: INSIDE INFO

Hidden gem If you are here in spring, look out for processional caterpillars nesting in the aleppo pines behind the beaches. Although toxic to touch, the caterpillars are fascinating to watch.

Roman Pollentia

For an understanding of Mallorca's early history, visit the Roman city of Pollentia (meaning "power"), founded on the site of present-day Alcúdia after the conquest of Mallorca in 123 BC. Settlers were brought over from mainland Spain, at that time the Roman province of Hispania; Christianity and the Latin language were introduced, and the Talaiotic culture gradually suppressed.

Pollentia remained a powerful city for some 500 years, until its inhabitants moved to modern-day Pollença and named it after their old capital. The ruins of Pollentia are the only significant Roman remains on Mallorca; most of them can be found in a small area to the south of Sant Jaume Church in Alcúdia.

The Bridge

The Pont Roma, which is actually situated on the outskirts of Pollença and not in Roman Pollentia, spans the Sant Jordi torrent which carries water only when it washes down from the mountains after heavy rain. The bridge belonged to the network of roads that the Romans built when they settled the island in 123 BC. The central pillar and one span date from the Imperial Age of Rome, while the rest has been rebuilt through the centuries. A few aqueduct arches, still standing on private land a kilometre north, were part of the system that transported water from a mountain spring to the Roman town of Pollentia (now Alcúdia) 14km southeast.

Spring rain-water fills the stream beneath Pollentia's Roman bridge

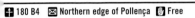

✚ 180 B4   ✉ Northern edge of Pollença   🆓 Free

TAKING A BREAK

From the plain but friendly Bar Pont Roma near by (Carrer Bartomeu Aloy 24, tel: 971 532485), you can look out through the slender cypresses to the grey-stone mountains beyond. The bar serves good coffee. Tasty *tapas* include pork with wild mushrooms, chicken wings and chopped fried liver.

Museu Monogràfic de Pollentia

Housed in a small Gothic hospital dating from the 14th century, this museum gives an interesting insight into the daily life of ancient Rome. Displays include an array of pottery pieces, some imported from other areas of the empire for domestic use, farm tools, surgical instruments, game pieces and jewellery made from bone. There are also clay oil lamps, theatrical masks and objects used in home worship of ancestors. The most outstanding sculptures are the veiled bust of Augustus, the bronze head of a young girl and a white marble statue of a military officer wearing a breastplate decorated with mythological images. A bronze tablet dating from 10 BC describes how the Talaiot town of Bocchoris was successfully being absorbed by the Roman Empire.

The tombstone of Callus Asinius, a banished Roman traitor, was found in the old town

✚ 180 C4 ✉ Carrer Sant Jaume 30, Alcúdia ☎ 971 547004 🕓 Tue–Fri 10–1:15, 3:30–5:15, Sat–Sun 10:30–12:45
💷 Inexpensive

The Town

Pollentia reached its peak in the 1st century BC and the Romans were the first to bring urban life to Mallorca: they cultivated grapes and planted olive trees. The old walled town covered 12ha. The excavated area gives an idea of the layout of the town, including two residences, House of Two Treasures, with several rooms built around a central atrium where two caches of bronze coins were unearthed, and the Bronze Head House, the largest home of all (700sq m), where the bronze head of a young girl was found in 1948. Arcade Street, between these two houses, was once covered by a roof resting on columns. Many items found during excavation are on display in the museum in Alcúdia.

✚ 180 C4 ✉ Opposite church of Sant Jaume and city walls, Alcúdia
🕓 Tue–Fri 10–1:15, 3:30–5:15, Sat–Sun 10:30–12:45
💷 Inexpensive

The Gym and the Forum

These are still being excavated and you can see them only from the rock-walled trail that runs from the Roman town to the theatre. The gym was 30m long and ten plinths which once supported columns have been dug up.

Various statues and inscribed stones have been dug up in the forum, or public square, which measured 26m in width. Here was a temple dedicated to the gods Jupiter (war), Minerva (wisdom and technology) and Juno (marriage). There were also two smaller temples, a few shops and possibly a law court.

The Theatre

Built on a hillside two millennia ago and used for 200 years, this is the smallest Roman theatre (about 75m in diameter) found in Spain. It held 2,500 spectators and was used primarily for theatrical drama, not gladiator fights or wild animal shows. The ten tiers of seats in semicircular design, the orchestra and the rectangular stage (with five holes to fit in a wooden platform) are still relatively intact. If you want to make a speech or sing, stand centre stage: the acoustics are excellent. At the back of the theatre are prehistoric caves, and carved into the stone seats are several medieval burial tombs, trapezoidal in shape. Theatre excavation started in 1952.

If you use your imagination you can still hear Roman crowds at the theatre

✚ 180 C4 ✉ Located 0.5km off the Alcúdia–Port d'Alcúdia road (C-713) 🕐 Always open ✋ Free

ROMAN POLLENTIA: INSIDE INFO

Hidden gem When the Catalan Christians took over the island in the 13th century, they immediately started building churches. One of their first still stands: the Oratori Santa Anna (open mornings only), a few hundred metres down the road south past the Roman ruins, was built in Gothic style in the 13th century. Above the entrance is a stone carving of the Virgin and Child holding the dove of peace in his hands. During the 17th century, the oratory was used as a hospital for sick sailors. The Santa Anna Fiesta on 8 September features a procession and horse and foot racing near by. The chapel is lovely in its simplicity.

Alcúdia and Port d'Alcúdia

Hidden behind the solid defensive walls of this busy tourist town is a perfectly preserved old quarter where Renaissance palaces shelter in narrow, shady streets. Once the Roman capital of Pollentia, Alcúdia was sacked by the Vandals and returned to greatness under the Moors, who named it *al-kudia* ("small hill" in Arabic). The Spanish built the medieval ramparts, symbol of the town, while in the 20th century the port district has grown from a small fishing harbour into a busy commercial port and the biggest resort area on the east coast.

The tower of the town hall in Alcúdia stands guard over the town

The two towns are on the rise of land that separates the bays of Pollença and Alcúdia – it's 9km from one end of Alcúdia to the other. In both towns cars are prohibited from their most attractive streets, consequently you can enjoy strolling through the compact core of rejuvenated old Alcúdia, and in ultra-modern Port d'Alcúdia you can follow the palms and pines along the new promenade from the fishing port to the beginning of the beaches.

A shuttle train (inexpensive) runs through the resort town from Port d'Alcúdia south to S'Albufera in summer.

The Walls

Alcúdia has two rings of walls, one medieval built about 700 years ago and the outer Renaissance wall dating from the 17th century. The walls were declared a historic-artistic monument in 1963, but the inner wall was subsequently almost entirely rebuilt. The medieval arched gates and square towers of Xara or Moll and Mallorca or Sant Sebastià, the main gate looking out to the road to Palma, are largely original. You can also see a remnant of the moat. All that remains of the outer fortification is Sant Ferran now housing the 100-year-old bullring (mock bullfights are staged on Thursday afternoons in summer; other events include rock and pop concerts) and a few wall sections.

✚ 180 C4   🎟 Free

The Library

Alcúdia is proud home to a beautiful library, built within a
lovingly restored 500-year-old Renaissance-style mansion. The
Can Torro Library is open to all, and you can relax and read a
newspaper, check your email or admire the sculptures in the
exquisite inner courtyard. The library opened in 1990, funded
by City Hall and the German Bertelsmann Foundation. The
adjacent Can Fondo sports the city's oldest coat of arms.

**The port gate
was originally
erected in
1298**

Church of San Jaume

The stark San Jaume Parish Church, the tallest building in
Alcúdia town, was originally erected in the early-14th century.
A substantial part of it collapsed in 1870, but was rebuilt
shortly thereafter. Above the front entrance is an image of St
James, the patron saint of both Spain and Alcúdia. In a niche
to the side of the main chapel stands a wood carving of the

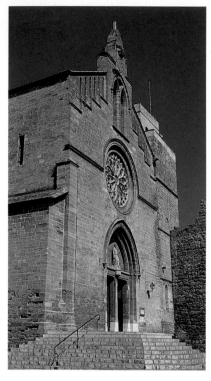

San Jaume Church is a landmark of the northeast coast

Holy Christ from around 1500. In 1507 the region suffered a drought so severe that the townspeople carried the statue to nearby Cove Sant Marti, a cave with an altar, and prayed for rain. According to legend, the carving sweated blood and water. The rains came, the crops were saved and the chapel was built to house the sacred statue.

The Port

The port comprises the commercial docks to the north (where containers of goods are unloaded for distribution around the island), the fishermen's wharf and a modern marina of luxury yachts flying flags from all over the world. South of the port stretches one of biggest and best beaches (► 115) on the island. Extending inland and along the coast from the marina is a vast congregation of hotel and apartment complexes, restaurants and shops of every description, and the greatest number of dark-to-dawn discos east of Palma. You can take your pick of ear-numbing music at Menta (► 132), countless karaoke bars or entertainers who perform frequently in various Port d'Alcúdia hotels.

TAKING A BREAK

Plaça Constitució, near City Hall, has several cafés where you can sit in the sun, watch the town walk past and re-energise.

ALCÚDIA AND PORT D'ALCÚDIA: INSIDE INFO

Top tips Children love the excitement of the go-kart track, as well as the Hidropark (tel: 971 891672; open daily 10–6, May–Oct) with its numerous water slides, boating pools and 54 holes of mini-golf.

• A good way to see the two towns of Alcúdia, along with the Roman ruins, is by bicycle. The area is relatively flat, there are several designated cycle trails and you'll have no parking problems.

Hidden gem A drive across Cap de Pinar, the headland separating Pollença and Alcúdia bays, leads to the remote 17th-century hermitage of La Victoria, a fortress-like church and a centre of pilgrimage with views over the bay.

Artà and Ses Països

The historic town of Artà is dominated by its church and castle, situated within the medieval walls on a 180-m high hill. Humans have been living here for at least 3,000 years, as evidenced by the Bronze-Age settlement of Ses Països just outside the town. The castle was originally a Roman barracks, later an Arab fortress and then a Christian temple. Today the town is best known for its raffia basketware, with espadrilles, hats and baskets on sale at the Saturday craft market and the weekly market on Tuesdays.

It's worth the ten-minute trek to the top of the town and the Santuari de Sant Salvador, not only for the panoramic view over the roof-tops and the fields of pigs and horses among the trees, but also to see the sanctuary itself, with its portraits of two Mallorcan heroes, Jaume the Conqueror and Ramón Llull. To get there, start at the town hall and walk up to the parish church of Transfiguració del Senyor, then climb the steps between an avenue of cypress trees to reach the sanctuary. The

Ses Països
- ✚ 181 E3   ✉ 2km south of Artà
- ☎ 619 070010
- 🕐 Daily 10–7, in summer; 10–5, in winter
- 🎫 Inexpensive

The view over the terracotta roofs of Artà from Sant Salvadore Sanctuary

The hilltop fortress at Artà covers an area of 4,000sq m

simple bar at the top makes a marvellous paella and also sells souvenirs. While you are there, take a walk around the battlements, with their stone towers and solid defensive walls.

There are more walls at Ses Païsses, 2km south of Artà, the most representative and best-preserved Bronze-Age settlement on the island. The entire complex is surrounded by a massive Cyclopean wall, so called because of the belief that it must have been built by giants. Inside the wall, around 60 stone apartments were inhabited from 1200 BC until the Romans arrived a millennium later. The main entrance, still in use today, is formed from great blocks of stone weighing up to 8 tonnes each.

In the oak grove at the entrance to Ses Païsses stands a lichen-blackened monument to revered island bishop, poet and writer Miguel Costa i Llobera. In 1900 he was inspired by Ses Païsses to write *The Legacy of the Greek Genius*, an epic poem about a ritual sacrifice here. Priestess Nuredduna, granddaughter of the High Priest of the local Talaiotic tribe, fell in love with a Greek wanderer and his music. He was Homer, and he had been wrongly accused by the Talaiot people and was sentenced to death. But, while he was playing his lyre before being sacrificed, Nuredduna persuaded officials to let him die slowly in a cave instead. During the night, she crept to his cave and set him free. He escaped, but left his lyre behind. Her people soon discovered what she had done. She was stoned to death, hugging Homer's lyre, a symbol of her love for him and his music. This poem was adapted as an opera in 1947 with the name of *Nuredduna*.

Inside the village gate, the trail is well signposted. The central talaiot (watch-tower), dating from 1200 BC, is the oldest structure in the town. In the foundations in one of the rooms flanking the main talaiot is a brazier cut in stone, where live coals were kept from day to day. The three rectangular rooms were probably for living quarters and the horseshoe-shaped room for cremations.

TAKING A BREAK

Hike or drive up the hill in the centre of Artà to the Sant Salvador Café (Plaça Sant Salvador, s/n) for a delicious paella.

ARTÀ AND SES PAÏSSES: INSIDE INFO

In more depth Objects uncovered in excavation preserved in the Artà Museum include ceramic pieces, small objects in stone and bone, and copper and bronze tools. Also in the museum are other Ses Païsses items, such as oil lamps and figurines, probably brought back from the Punic Wars (264–146 BC) by Talaiotic Mallorcan mercenaries hired for their superb skill in targeting animals and people with slingshots. The museum is currently closed for repairs and may reopen in 2005.

Modern visitors use the same entrance to Ses Païsses as the Talaiot people did 3,000 years ago

At Your Leisure

❶ Pollença

Despite its popularity with expatriates and foreign artists, Pollença remains a typically Mallorcan town, at its best on Sunday mornings when the main square is the setting for a lively and colourful market. A prime attraction is the long flight of broad stone steps, with stately cypresses standing on either side, from the centre of town up Calvary Hill to a chapel at the top. The reward is a spectacular view of the town, the surrounding valleys and mountains, and the sea to the east.

Pollençines have always been patrons of the arts and consequently there are several good art galleries and interesting original works of art in banks, cafés and other public buildings. The summer music festival attracts top-notch musicians from all over the world to concerts held in the beautiful old Santo Domingo cloister. For an inside look at local art and one of Pollença's grand old houses, visit the Museu Dionis Bennàssar, named after Dionis Bennàssar (1904–67), the artist who once lived there. This elegant 17th-century home, marked with a large red banner hanging in front, has been lovingly restored and is filled with Bennàssar's vibrant landscapes, seascapes and peoplescapes from the Pollença area. At noon on an off-season Saturday, you can enjoy a short musical concert while you admire the Impressionist art. Afterwards, the museum offers complimentary apéritifs.

✚ 181 B4 ✉ Carrer Roca 14, Pollença

The Calvary steps now stretch into the town

☎ 971 530997
🕐 Tue–Sun 11–1
💷 Inexpensive

❷ Coves de l'Alzinaret

These ancient burial caves on the outskirts of Cala Sant Vicenç, first studied in 1927 by a British archaeologist, are among the few remnants of the pre-Talaiotic culture which existed on Mallorca before 1500 BC. On the corner of the first street to the left, a tall birch tree and a 2-m high talaiot mark the entrance to the hill park where there are six caves open to the public. A sign explains the history of these burial sites for pre-Talaiotic or Middle Bronze-Age people from around 1700–1400 BC. Follow the rocky footpath to the right through the pine, carob and evergreen oak trees to the first of four elongated caves, about a one-minute walk away. These four caves, located one after the other along this short trail, were made by Bronze-Age people, but tell little about life in pre-Talaiotic times because excavation treasures have been removed to the museum in Pollença.

The caves have small rectangular yards chiselled out of stone in front, then narrow passageways reminiscent of Inuit igloos lead to the mortuary chambers back inside the hillside. Skeletons with knees tucked up in the foetal position have been found in some of the small rectangular hollows (about 1m in length) carved into the

limestone inside. The last two caves, which are rounded, are believed to have been dwelling places.

➕ 180 B5 ✉ Signposted off road from Pollença to Cala Sant Vicenç
💷 Free

❻ Muro

This small town at the centre of Mallorca's main agricultural area is chiefly of interest because of its ethnological museum, a branch of the Museu de Mallorca in Palma. The Museu Etnòlogic is housed in a 17th-century mansion and consists mostly of re-creations of rooms, such as a kitchen, pharmacy and blacksmith's workshop, from earlier times. One of the most interesting exhibits is the collection of *siurells*, the clay whistles in the shape of humans and animals which have been manufactured in Mallorca for 1,000 years. Another feature of Muro is its unique bullring, built out of white stone in its own quarry in 1910 and still used for occasional fights.

➕ 180 B3 ✉ Carrer Major 15
☎ 971 717540 🕐 Tue–Sat 10–7, Sun 10–2 💷 Inexpensive

❽ Capdepera

The crenellated walls of a 14th-century castle dominate the landscape between Artà and the coast. If you are visiting Artà, it is well worth driving the few extra kilometres to Capdepera and climbing the steps to the castle from the main square. From the battlements there is a good view of Cala Ratjada (► 116), a busy water-sports resort at Mallorca's most easterly point. South of Capdepera, a minor road leads to the Coves d'Artà (► 141), which are marginally less visited but every bit as spectacular as the better-known Coves del Drac (► 138).

➕ 180 E3
☎ Castle: 971 818746
🕐 Daily 10–8, Apr–Oct; 10–5, rest of year 💷 Inexpensive

Where to... Stay

Prices

Prices are for the least expensive double room in high season, IVA sales tax included. Prices may drop by up to 50 per cent in low season. Breakfast is usually included in the room price. € = under 60 Euros €€ = 60–120 Euros €€€ = over 120 Euros

Aparthotel Flora €

Friendly staff, an in-house bar/café, a swimming-pool, a short stroll from a sandy beach and splendid mountain tableaux from the north make this apartment hotel a favourite with hikers and bikers all year round. The one-bedroom apartments, with living-room divans that sleep two more, all have balconies. Compact kitchenettes comprise a fridge, two timed electric burners and a toaster-oven. There is a daily maid service.

🔢 180 B5 ✉ Carrer Méndez Núñez, Port de Pollença
☎ 971 866176; fax: 971 866322

Apartamentos Marina €

These modernised seafront units, with spectacular bay views, may be the best bargain on the island, but you'd better book well in advance. Located right in the town centre, it's a two-minute walk to a beach, a newsagent, the marina and a fleet of stores, cafés, bars and restaurants. There is a daily maid service.

🔢 180 B5 ✉ Passeig Anglada Camarasa 7, Port de Pollença ☎ 971 867143; fax: 971 865093

Hostal Bahía €€

You can't go wrong at this little hotel, mainly because it's a family

business and the owners are almost always here seeing that customers are contented. Located on the beach on the Pine Walk, a five-minute stroll from the centre of town, the Bahía offers all modern conveniences, and has a popular beachfront restaurant under the pines. An unexpected bonus is the array of Mallorcan antiques incorporated into the décor.

🔢 180 B5 ✉ Passeig Voramar 17, Port de Pollença ☎ 971 866562; fax: 971 865630

Illa d'Or Hotel €€€

This grand old dame has been around since 1929 and continues to successfully combine tradition and comfort with an exquisite bayfront setting. The hotel has a beach, a dock, a heated indoor pool and Jacuzzi, an outdoor pool, gym and sauna. It's a lovely 10-minute stroll along the Pine Walk to the town centre. Even if you're not staying here, you can enjoy a sundowner on the waterfront terrace.

🔢 180 B5 ✉ Passeig Colom 265, Port de Pollença ☎ 971 865100; fax: 971 864213; email: illador@fehm.es; www.hoposa.es

La Moraleja Hotel €€€

Located in little Cala Sant Vicenç where the Tramuntana slopes down to meet the sea, this small hidden treasure is filled with original art and antiques, and features a collection of vintage cars. All 17 rooms are in an outbuilding annexed to the sumptuous lounges in the main villa. In case the beaches are too crowded, there are two swimming-pools with sun terraces in the spacious gardens.

🔢 180 B5 ✉ Avinguda Cavall Bernat, Cala Sant Vicenç
☎ 971 533010; fax: 971 533418 email: lamoraleja@fehm.es; www.lamoraleja.net

Parc Natural Hotel €€€

You will enjoy the broad, white, sandy beach, spectacular views, pools and spa, fine Mallorcan sculptures as part of the palatial décor,

Where to...
Eat and Drink

Prices

The € amount indicates what you can expect to pay per person for a meal, excluding drinks, tax and tip. € = under 15 Euros €€ = 15–30 Euros €€€ = over 30 Euros

Balada del Agua del Mar €€

While the chef keeps the kitchen humming, ever-cheerful partner Pierre waits on the red-chequered-clothed tables under the shade of a large fig tree. The grilled pork chops are tender and juicy, and the hearty fish soup is among the best around. The terrace looks out to a passing parade of people along the Pine Walk and to the beach and bay a few metres away. Although the interior is filled with an eclectic collection of Asian antiques, the outside tables are the coveted ones.

🚹 180 B5 ☒ Passeig Vora Mar 5, Port de Pollença ☎ 971 864276 🕐 Daily noon–3:30, 6–10, Apr–Oct

Bar El Casinet €€

This may be the best bar/café on the whole island – it has sunny seafront tables and sunny service day or night. Coffee comes with a chocolate or biscuit sampler, and the variety of sandwiches will please any palate. Inside, there's a big-screen TV, a dartboard, two pool tables and lively recorded music.

🚹 180 B5 ☒ Anglada Camarassa 15, Port de Pollença ☎ 971 866394 🕐 Daily 8:30 am–4 am, in summer

Bar Pedro €

Affable expatriate hosts Giles and Robert serve sandwiches and *tapas* to a steady flow of artists, writers and other eccentrics. The best time to come is after Pollença Sunday market, when Robert makes the meanest Bloody Marys in town.

🚹 180 B4 ☒ Carrer Cecilio Metelo 38, Pollença ☎ 971 531565 🕐 Wed–Mon 9:30–3, 7–11

Bar Pont Roma €

This unpretentious bar/café on the western side of Pollença gives a warm welcome. Although the *tapas* selection is limited (you can enjoy meatballs, bread, olives and wine for a song), the view from a window booth out to the eastern fringe of the Tramuntana feeds the soul.

🚹 180 B4 ☒ Carrer Bmé Aloy 24, Pollença ☎ 971 532485 🕐 Early morning until the last customer leaves

Café Juma €

The main square of Pollença is lined with cafés and restaurants which

---

complimentary evening entertainment several times weekly, good food and super service. If you like birdwatching, this hotel is on the edge of S'Albufera swamp (▶ 165), one of the best ornithological regions in Europe, but remember that some of the birds are here because they like to snack on mosquitoes.

🚹 180 C4 ☒ Platja de Muro, Carretera Port d'Alcúdia–Artà ☎ 971 892017; fax: 971 890345

Sis Pins €€

This charming *belle époque* hotel is ablaze with bougainvillaea climbing the arches of the arcaded seafront terrace. Be sure to request a waterfront room when you book. Sis Pins was discovered by the cast of British TV soap *Coronation Street* when the show first hit the screen, and Agatha Christie stayed here long before that when she wrote a short story about Pollença Bay (▶ 30).

🚹 180 B5 ☒ Passeig Anglada Camarasa 77, Port de Pollença ☎ 971 867050; fax: 971 866264

come alive each Sunday after the weekly market. Locals gather outside the Club Pollença and Café Espanyol, but for a wide choice of *tapas* head for this recently renovated hotel, which has been in the same family since 1907. Choose a chair on the terrace and tuck into a selection of delicious *tapas* ranging from *pa arb oli* with ham to garlic potatoes, seafood salad, meatballs and chicken croquettes. The hotel is decorated with artworks by Aina Cifre, the daughter of the current owner.

Café Mestral €€

🕂 180 B4 ☒ Plaça Major 9, Pollença ☎ 971 533258 🕒 Tue–Sun 8 am–10 pm

A goblet of freshly squeezed orange juice, a fluffy breakfast bun, *café con leche*, the morning newspaper, lively waiters, watchful management and a seaside location – does life get any better than this? For lunch or dinner, opt for one of the various thin-crust pizzas for which the

Mestral is famous. Café Mestral also owns the Baskin-Robbins ice-cream franchise next door.

🕂 180 B5 ☒ Passeig Anglada Camarassa 63, Port de Pollença ☎ 971 864098 🕒 Tue–Sun 9 am until late, Mar–Nov

Clivia Restaurant €€

Behind the long lace curtains framing terracotta pots of clivia, white walls sport original oils of sea- and landscapes. Mini-appetisers of mountain ham and bread with creamy Asturian butter arrive automatically. The earthenware tureen of steaming saffroned broth is studded with squid, octopus, whitefish and little islands of bread fried in olive oil. The mixed romaine salad is one of the tastiest bargains around.

🕂 180 B4 ☒ Avinguda Pollentia, Pollença ☎ 971 533635 🕒 Thu–Tue 1–3, 7–10

El Posito €

Go where the locals go for the big midday meal, the bargain of the

decade. For the price of a cocktail at an up-market hotel, here you can enjoy the *menú del día*, a hefty three-course meal with wine. The first course may be a choice between stew and pasta, the second between grilled pork loin or sole. Dessert choices include flan, pudding or ice-cream. With so much fuel, you may feel like cycling over the pass to Formentor, or you may simply take a short stroll to the beach to sleep it off. El Posito specialises in rice dishes and mussels.

🕂 180 B5 ☒ Carrer Llebeig 8, Port de Pollença ☎ 971 865413 🕒 Sun–Fri 12:30–3:30, 7–11

Ivy Garden €€€

British expatriate entrepreneurs Keely and Billy have combined culinary expertise with the right recipe of elegance and informality to create a magnet for the trendy zest-for-life media and fashion world, largely from London. The spinach soufflé tantalises the taste buds enough to make you want to try the

honey-roasted suckling pig flavoured with sage and served with fresh vegetables in season. A cosy palm-shaded patio beats the heat of summer.

🕂 180 B5 ☒ Carrer Llevant 14, Port de Pollença ☎ 971 866271 🕒 Daily 7 pm–11 pm, Mar–mid-Dec

L'Aup €€€

Chef José González is a perfectionist and it shows. The bouillabaise is so good that you may not have room for the immaculate sea bass or grilled loin of pork; the leg of spring lamb is enormous. There is a shaded terrace for summer dining and an intriguing collection of old carriages and farm tools in the yard.

🕂 180 B4 ☒ Carretera Port de Pollença–Pollença at Cala Sant Vicenç turnoff ☎ 971 532606 🕒 Thu–Tue 1–3:30, 7–11:30

Luna de Miel €€

Who would expect to find a good Chinese restaurant with great bay and marina views in a Spanish resort? At the entrance, a fat gilded Buddha points your way upstairs. Although there are many dishes to choose from, you can't go wrong with the sweet and sour soup, aubergines with tofu, chicken with almonds or fried pork with Chinese mushrooms. You can take any left-over food home for breakfast.

➕ 180 B5 ⊠ Passeig Saralegui 1, Port de Pollença ☎ 971 867061 🕐 Daily noon–4, 6–midnight

Stay €€€

This seafood restaurant on the harbour jetty definitely wins the vote for the most romantic dinner spot in Port de Pollença. The fish comes straight from the fishing port and is always fresh, whether it is hake, sole or fillets of grouper in *salsa verde*. If you're not sure what to order, try the *parrillada*, a delicious mixed grill of fish and seafood.

➕ 180 B5 ⊠ Moll Nou, Port de Pollença ☎ 971 864013 🕐 Daily 12:30–4, 7–10:30

Where to... Shop

No matter in which East Coast resort you are based, there is always a string of shops sporting beach towels, T-shirts, leather goods, perfumes and ceramics. Some shops stay open late in summer to accommodate after-dinner strollers.

Local Specialities

Lina (Economo Torres 5, Port de Pollença) has some of the best prices for leather (bags, belts, slippers, shoes) on the island. Bargains are often remaindered items from bigger stores. Their other store (Economo Torres 25) has a more elaborate array of up-market leather goods. **Xics & Xiques** (Carrer Migjorn 3, Port de Pollença) has a good array of clothes for children.

The **Ensenat** deli (Roger de Lauria 10, Port de Pollença) has been selling *sobrasada* and cheese for 50 years: try their barbecued chicken for a picnic at the beach.

Clothes

Forget your bathing suit? **Bon Temps** (Passeig Saralegui 10, Port de Pollença), on the seafront sports a wide variety of inexpensive beach and swimwear, big beach towels, sun hats, shorts and casual dresses.

Crafts

Some beautiful crafts originate in this region: they're expensive but they will last almost for ever. **Casa Maria** (Passeig Saralegui 86, Port de Pollença) has been famous for hand embroideries for decades. Curly stylised leaves and flowers in strong blues, reds and greens on white linen adorn tablecloths, napkins, place mats and dresser runners.

Galeries Vicenç, on the roundabout northeast of Pollença, is famous for *roba de llengues* heavy cotton drapery fabric (it's durable but challenging to iron) and authentic Mallorcan furniture from centuries past. **Mestre Paco**, both next door and on the other side of the roundabout, also has a fabulous selection of old furniture and antique *objets d'art*.

Artà is famous for hats, mats, baskets and fans made from raffia palm. They're sold at many stores around the island, but the Saturday craft market in Artà might be more fun. If you miss the market, the little **Can Pantali** shop (Carrer Toni Blanes 21) has raffia work made by the shopkeeper.

East Coast Markets

Tuesday Alcúdia
Wednesday Port de Pollença
Friday Can Picafort
Saturday Cala Ratjada
Sunday Pollença

Where to...
Be Entertained

Visitors to this area generally entertain themselves swimming, walking, cycling and hiking during the day, then fall asleep after a leisurely evening meal. Nevertheless, there is no shortage of cultural activities.

Night-life

In Port de Pollença, Coconuts (next door to the Ivy Garden, tel: 971 864953) is the most popular spot for late-night drinks and music. At the Chivas Discotheque (tel: 971 866001), the beat hasn't changed in 30 years, but people still love it. After midnight, night owls head to Port d'Alcúdia, where la movida carries on at several discos until dawn. Menta (on Avenida Tucan, tel: 971 891972), a popular disco which

is open all year (weekends only in winter), has several floors of bars, laser shows, and even a swimming-pool for cooling down. Atoms is also popular, but Magic takes the biscuit. In Can Picafort, Skau (which means "trick" and "cave" in Mallorquin) is another popular night-owl haunt.

Concerts

The renowned Pollença Music Festival (tel: 971 534012; www.festivalpollenca.org) is held during July and August. The festival was founded in 1962 by the British violinist Philip Newman. Such top-notch international artists as Thomas Moser, Martin Mastik, Isaac Stern and Monserrat Caballé perform under the stars in the 16th-century cloister.

Outdoor Activities

Mallorca Balloons (tel: 971 818182), in Cala Ratjada, offer half-hour and hour-long rides high in the sky, over Manacor and Petra. David Yazdan (tel: 971 585803) in Cala Millor, rents microlights during the summer.

Bird-watching and Hiking

These are both popular pastimes in and around Pollença and Alcúdia. The tourist office in Cala Ratjada organises free half-day walks/hikes every Sunday.

Cycling

Cycling here is popular with casual cyclists as well as with more serious bicycle fans. Designated cycle trails link Port de Pollença with Pollença and Alcúdia. Cycle paths also run south from Port d'Alcúdia to Can Picafort, where you can sidetrack to the bird-watching trails in S'Albufera swamp. Cycling the meandering country roads is a good way to see the back-country homes and gardens, farms and fields.

Fiesta Fun

The most famous fiesta of the East Coast is probably the mock battle between the Moors and the Christians in Pollença on 2 August every year. Locals re-enact that night in 1550 when Pollencines chased the Moors out of town.

Golf

There are nine-hole golf-courses near Pollença and Son Servera. In the Artà area, the Canyamel, Capdepera and Pula courses all have 18 holes.

Sailing

Sailors and windsurfers love Pollença Bay, especially the breezes that often spring up on short notice. You can sign up for instruction for an hour, a day or a week, or you can hire any equipment you need and head out on your own. Sail & Surf (on the waterfront in Port de Pollença) has 25 years of experience (Paseo Saralegui 134; tel: 971 865346; fax: 971 865953; www.sailsurf-pollensa.de.

Inland and South

Getting Your Bearings

With its almond groves, vineyards, villages and market towns, the fertile plain at the centre of the island is typical of Mallorca before the tourists took over. The coach parties may flock into Inca and Manacor in search of leather and artificial pearls, but for the most part this area goes about its business largely unaffected by the crowds on the coast. Farmstays and country hotels are gradually opening up, and wealthy Spaniards and foreigners are buying up many of the agricultural estates, but this is still the best place on the island to catch that elusive and somewhat mythical quality, "the real Mallorca".

The best way to explore Es Pla (the plain) is simply to meander along the country lanes, many of which were first laid out in Roman times. You pass windmills, orchards and almond groves, one of the most beautiful sights in Mallorca when they carpet the ground with a layer of delicate white blossom each February. You stumble across small towns, with huge sandstone churches and rows of green-shuttered houses in narrow streets. The flat landscape is dotted with hills, many of them crowned with sanctuaries offering peace and magnificent views.

South of the plain, the coast from S'Arenal to Porto Cristo varies from broad sandy beaches like Es Trenc (popular with nudists) to fjords like Cala Figuera. There are busy holiday resorts like Cala d'Or with its glitzy marina and Porto Cristo with its family attractions, but much of the coastline in between is a rugged shore of remote beaches and creeks, some of which can only be reached by boat. The salt marshes at Ses Salines are known for their birdlife, while the island of Cabrera is an offshore wilderness and a haven for wildlife ranging from seabirds to lizards and Mediterranean turtles.

Outdoor living is one of the biggest attractions of the Mediterranean

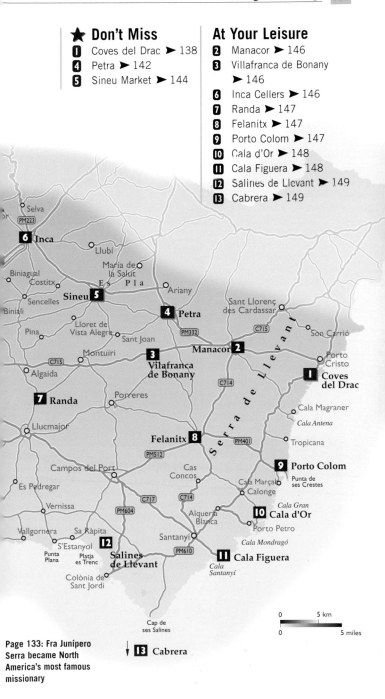

★ Don't Miss

At Your Leisure

Page 133: Fra Junípero Serra became North America's most famous missionary

Caves, cellars, country roads…and a pair of historic monasteries where you can spend the night. It is best to start this trip on Tuesday, if you can, to fit in with Sineu's weekly market.

Inland and South In Two Days

Day 1

Morning

Try to arrive early at the Coves del Drac (pictured right, ➤ 138) to avoid the queues and the crowds. After the tour, head down to Porto Cristo for an hour on the beach before lunch at one of the fish restaurants overlooking the harbour.

Afternoon

Make the short journey to Manacor (➤ 146) to visit a pearl factory and shop for carved olive-wood souvenirs at Oliv-Art (such as the one pictured left). Continue to Petra (➤ 142) for the Junípero Serra house and museum. After a drink in the main square, walk or drive the 4km to Ermita de Bonany for fabulous views over the plain. The church takes its name from the *bon any* (good year) of 1609, when the villagers climbed the hill to pray for rain and saw their prayers answered.

Evening

If you are feeling adventurous, you could spend the night at Bonany In one of the simple whitewashed cells. There is no food, so pick up a picnic in the village or have an early dinner at Sa Creu (➤ 152) on the outskirts of Petra.

Day 2

Morning

Drive to Sineu (➤ 144) for the weekly market, then continue to Inca (➤ 146) for lunch in one of its cellar restaurants (pictured above). After lunch, you may want to hunt for bargains in Inca's leather factories and showrooms.

Afternoon

Enjoy a leisurely drive across the plain and back down the east coast. A minor road from Inca leads through Sencelles on its way to Algaida, where you could make a small diversion to visit the Gordiola glass factory (glass pictured right), in a mock castle on the Palma to Manacor road. Continue to Randa (➤ 147) and take the winding road up the hillside to the sanctuary at the summit. Afterwards, follow the country roads through Llucmajor and Porreres to Felanitx (➤ 147), where another winding trail leads to the Santuari de Sant Salvador (➤ 151), with comfortable rooms and views stretching from Cabrera to Formentor. If you don't want to eat in the monastery, make the short journey to Porto Colom (➤ 147) for a dinner of fresh fish on the quayside.

Coves del Drac

Do not be put off by the crowds outside these vast underground caves, which have deservedly become one of Mallorca's most visited attractions. Although the demands of tourism have changed the way we see the caves, they remain just as remarkable and mysterious as when they were first explored in the 19th century.

In 1867, the Archduke Luis Salvador of Austria (► 101), who left his court to settle in Mallorca for a lifetime of research and writing, immortalised these caves in his book *Die Balearen*. The name, Dragon Caves, comes from the medieval myth of a bat-winged dragon with the body of a snake which was the resident guardian of any treasures hidden in these caves.

The hour-long tour, guided in five languages, begins with a descent down into the ground and along a roped trail comprising 700m of artistically lit underground panoramas. Stalagmites build up and stalactites inch down, sometimes meeting in the middle to form Roman-style grooved columns. Watch for the leaning tower of Pisa, the monk, the castle in ruins, the flag and other intriguing formations. Alongside the walkway are several pools of water, varying from 5m to 8m in depth, where strings of lime link like strands of pearls and appear as coral outcroppings in the crystal-clear salt water.

The tour stops at the underground theatre overlooking a lake about 177m long and 30m wide, where a narrator describes the history and geological features of the caves.

The lake is called Lake Martel, in honour of geologist Edward Alfred Martel who discovered it in 1896. He and the son of the cave owner, along with the grandson of Archduke Luis Salvador's lawyer who sponsored the expedition, sailed across this lake that same year in two fabric canoes.

Out of the darkness comes the sound of music: the lake is the stage for this theatre. One of a fleet of illuminated boats emerges from the blackness and weaves its way across the lake. A quartet of musicians aboard one boat is playing classical music. The sight of the lighted boats sailing between a ceiling forest of frosted needle stalactites and the reflections in the water provides an illusion of two forests with the boats appearing sometimes to float between the dual images.

The show as performed today started 70 years ago. For 47 years, the Drac Quartet was conducted by Jaume Vadell who has given 30,000 concerts on the lake. Many famous dancers, singers and other musicians have also performed in this memorable setting.

Ancient relics found in the caverns at Drac indicate that islanders have used the caves for thousands of years

➕ 181 E1
✉ Porto Cristo
☎ 971 820753
🕐 Daily: tours on the hour 10–5, Apr–Sep; tours at 10:45, noon, 2 and 3:30, rest of year 💶 Expensive

The stalactite ceiling rises to a dome 17m above Lake Martel

Electricity was installed in the caves in 1935, and a network of lights lit up the limestone, one of the earliest uses of artistic illumination in the world. The project was conceived and directed by engineer Carlos Buïgas (1898–1979) who achieved fame for his illuminated fountains at the Barcelona World Fair in 1929. Buïgas refused payment for his 15 months of work in the Drac Caves, saying, "This work is priceless, because there is none like it. Besides, I have enjoyed it because of all the challenges and difficult conditions I had to work under." Buïgas updated the installation in 1950, with 630m of submarine cable salvaged from the New York–London undersea cable. He later said that the Lake Martel illumination was the masterpiece of his life.

After the concert, you have the option of walking out or of making a short trip by boat along the lake to the path that leads to the exit. The boat trip is quite magical.

Other Caves

Mallorca has thousands of caves. You can visit these:

Artà
✚ 181 F3
✉ 8km southeast of Artà at Canyamel
☎ 971 841293
🕐 Daily 10–7, Jul–Sep; 10–5, rest of year
💷 Expensive

Campanet
✚ 180 A3
✉ 3km north of Campanet
☎ 971 516130
🕐 Daily 10–7, Apr–Sep; 10–6, rest of year
💷 Expensive

Génova
✚ 179 D2
✉ Carrer Barranç 45, Génova
☎ 971 402387
🕐 Daily 10–1:30, 4–7, in summer; Tue–Sun 11–1, 4–6, in winter
💷 Moderate

Hams
✚ 181 E1
✉ Porto Cristo
☎ 971 820988
🕐 Daily 10–6, Apr–Oct; 10:30–5, rest of year
💷 Expensive

COVES DEL DRAC: INSIDE INFO

Top tips If you're claustrophobic, visit the caves early in the day before the crowds of tour buses arrive or late in the day after they've gone. There is a large, free car-park in front of the caves.
• Some people, especially small children, might find the caves frightening. Once you are in, there is no easy way to get out, so think about this before you buy your tickets.
• Some of the paths are slippery, so remember to wear sensible shoes.

Hidden gem Children might also enjoy the small aquarium, which is situated across the car-park close to the caves.

Petra

Petra is a small town with a big claim to fame. With rows of sand-coloured houses in a neat grid of narrow streets, it is Mallorca's best remaining example of medieval town planning. However, it is best known as the birthplace of one of Mallorca's most illustrious sons, Fra Junípero Serra (1713–84).

On a little street down the lane from the Franciscan friary where Serra began his religious studies, stands the humble stone house where this founder of nine Californian missions was born. Perhaps the purposeful pioneer liked California because its climate and landscapes reminded him of his native island.

It's still amazing that Father Serra found his way so far west nearly 300 years ago and that he walked 3,000km to get there. Even today, when thousands of ramblers from all over Europe converge to walk the mountains, valleys and plains of this Mediterranean island, few find their way to Petra.

Fra Junípero's parents were island farmers

The whitewashed interior of the tiny two-storey Serra home comprises a parlour with primitive furnishings, a small kitchen with a walk-in fireplace, an adjoining stable for the family donkey, two small bedrooms and a large room

Serra Home and Museum
✚ 180 C2　✉ Carrer Barracar Alt 6–8
☎ 971 561149　🕐 Opening times vary, if closed ► Inside Info
💰 Donation requested

upstairs with hanging shelves for drying and storing such foodstuffs as tomatoes, peppers, cheese and sausage. The tiny back garden is a pocket of peace. The arched front doorway was in place at the time of Fra Serra's birth.

Beside the house, the Serra Centre includes a library and a museum chronicling the friar's life and times. A collection of paintings illustrates Spanish missionary work in New Spain.

Across the narrow street from the museum, the San Bernadino Convent may be opened upon request. The Romanesque interior is particularly interesting because of the baroque side chapels dedicated to saints. Father Serra named his Californian missions after these representations which include San Juan Capistrano, Santa Ana, San Diego and San Francisco. These missions and others are portrayed in nine tiled paintings on the pedestrian street in front of the museum.

Other sites of interest include the Gothic Parish Church where Serra was baptised and the Plaça Junipero Serra with its monument of the venerable friar. His statue is also in the Hall of Fame in Washington, DC.

TAKING A BREAK

Walk to the main *plaças* where the best spot for refreshment is Bar Els Arcs. The local pilgrim site is Bonany, a high hill crowned with a cross commemorating Father Serra's last sermon to the people of Petra before leaving for America. The hilltop looks out over the village houses with their tiny gardens and drystone walls and across the fertile farm fields and crumbling windmills to the azure sea.

The San Diego mission founded by the "Walking Friar" is still open to visitors today

Sineu Market

The Wednesday market in Sineu is one of the best and most traditional on the island. The earlier the hour the better the selection of produce, yet the pace picks up as the morning moves on. Flower stalls sell a blaze of roses, sweet peas, marigolds, dahlias, gladioli and cala lilies. A rainbow of multicoloured tarpaulins shades stalls selling fresh local produce, including the home-marinated bitter green olives typical of Mallorca.

Mallorcans come from all over the island to buy fresh duck for their Sunday meal

Most of the action takes place in the church square, Sa Plaça, where farmers sell sun-dried tomatoes, strings of garlic, cured sausages and bags full of snails. The market spills out of the plaza and along the side streets, where traders from Spain and Africa offer pottery, lace and ethnic crafts. Walk up the steps to see the statue of a winged lion, the symbol of Sineu, then wander down to a large open square, Plaça Es Fossar, where Mallorca's only remaining livestock market takes place. Also in this square are stalls specialising in new and used clothes and household items, and pavement cafés where you can watch the drama unfold. The market closes around noon, when the farmers drift off to the cellar restaurants for platefuls of *frit de porcella*, a local speciality of pork innards with vegetables and potatoes.

Sineu is located in the geographical centre of the island and in the heart of Es Pla, the fertile agricultural plain that produces up to

List of Weekly Markets

There are dozens of weekly markets held all round the island; most are held in the morning but be there early to see the best of the produce. Check with your local tourist information office to find a comprehensive list.

Monday Manacor
Tuesday Artà
Wednesday Sineu
Thursday Inca
Friday Can Picafort
Saturday Palma
Sunday Pollença

S'Estació Museum

✚ 180 B2 ✉ Carrer Estacio 2
☎ 971 520750
🕐 Mon–Fri 9:30–1:30, 4–7; Sat 9:30–1
💶 Free

An abundance of fresh produce creates a healthy Mediterranean diet

three crops a year. On the first Sunday in May the town plays host to a large agricultural fair, first held in 1319, where live-stock, chickens, vegetables, flowerpots, knives and saddles are all sold.

SINEU MARKET: INSIDE INFO

Top tips

• Go early to avoid the crowds who arrive mid-morning by tour bus.

• If you enjoy art, take time to visit the old train station which has been turned into a contemporary art museum – S'Estació.

At Your Leisure

Mallorca's manufactured pearls never lose their lustre

2 Manacor

Mallorca's second city is an industrial centre specialising in furniture-making and the fabricating of manufactured pearls. After the hourly tour of any of several pearl factories, you can purchase these beauties in earrings, necklaces, bracelets and other jewellery. It's almost impossible to distinguish these fish-scale and shellfish pearls from real ones, but the manufacturing process is labour intensive, costly and a closely guarded secret. You might also want to visit the Oliv-Art workshop and gift shop. Watch for the old olive trees and the life-size dinosaurs in front. Olive wood is becoming scarcer all the time, but it is very durable and the grain is attractive. A good buy is an olive-wood cutting board. Prices are about the same as you would pay at any island market.

Oliv-Art
✚ 181 D2
✉ Carretera Palma–Artà, Km 47
☎ 971 846261
◷ Daily 9–6

Majorica
✚ 181 D2
✉ Avinguda Majorica 48
☎ 971 550200
◷ Mon–Fri 9–6; Sat–Sun 9:30–12:30
💶 Free

Villafranca's September melon festival is a highlight of the town's year

3 Villafranca de Bonany

This small town on the road from Palma to Manacor has managed to draw attention to itself with its colourful shopfronts exhibiting local produce all along the main street. Braids of garlic, strands of red peppers (the smaller the pepper the sharper the flavour), tomatoes and sponges, along with extensive displays of gourds large, medium and small, announce the fascinating grocery shops. Melons grown in this neighbourhood are especially good thanks to the perfect combination of sun and soil. Prices are often better here than elsewhere on the island: you can pick up a bottle of good red table wine for a song and you won't even need a corkscrew to open it.
✚ 181 B1

6 Inca Cellers

A century ago, Inca had 60 *cellers* (bodegas), quiet, cool basements built partially underground to control temperature in which wine was made

place of pilgrimage ever since Ramón Llull established his first hermitage here in 1275.

The monastery, along with a big pale-green communications sphere, tops a ribbon of mountain ridges southeast of Palma. This distinctive landmark, at an altitude of 542m, sometimes serves as a reference point for the many pilots heading to Son Sant Joan Airport.

Follow the winding trail up the mountain to Nostra Senyora de Cura (Our Lady of Healing) on top. Little of the original 13th-century sanctuary remains. The main statue of the Virgin dates from the 15th century. In the loggia adjacent to the monastery church, glazed tiles depict the lives of Mary and Jesus. On a clear day you can see most of the island from here. There is a café and bar at the back of the monastery. But this site is most interesting because it was where 13th-century adventurer, mystic, scholar and missionary Ramón Llull retreated from the secular world (➤ 149).

🚹 182 B3

8 Felanitx

Although once known as an intellectual centre, Felanitx is today famous for pottery. Talented local artists transform the clay-like soil into beautiful ceramics, which are sold on the church steps during the Sunday morning market. Earthenware cooking pots and simple brown-glazed terracotta plates make good buys. Another place to browse and buy is the big ceramics shop Ceràmicas Mallorca, on the outskirts of town.

Ceràmicas Mallorca
🚹 182 D3
✉ Sant Agustín 50–58
☎ 971 580201
🕐 Mon–Fri 9–1 and 3–7;
Sat 10–1

9 Porto Colom

Colourful fishermen's huts and boathouses huddle around the quayside of this picturesque fishing village,

stored and sold. Workers developed the custom of bringing their midday bread and sausage here, so they could buy a glass of wine to wash it down. The few *cellers* that remain have evolved into fully-fledged restaurants specialising in classical Mallorcan cuisine. Enormous dark oak barrels, once used to age the wine, line the walls but now serve only as decoration. Each vat has a tiny rectangular doorway up high, just big enough for a small man to slip inside to clean it.

Some *cellers* are better than others. Celler Can Amer (➤ 151), whose large barrels have been here for 300 years, is the biggest and best. Local wines and the gastronomy of the land are married with efficient service under the watchful management of matriarch Antonia Cantallops. The open kitchen is decorated with a sparkling array of copper utensils once used for cooking. Other *cellers* near by are Sa Tavessa and Can Ripoll.

Celler Can Amer
🚹 180 A3
✉ Carrer Pau 39, Inca
☎ 971 501261
🕐 Mon–Sat 1–3:30, 7:30–11,
Sun 1–3:30

7 Randa

Situated at the highest point on the Mallorcan plain, the summit of Puig de Randa has been an important

pastel-coloured cottages set around small squares, and also contains the parish church. South of the harbour, the area around Cala Marçal has been developed into a modern beach resort and marina.

✚ 182 E3

🔟 Cala d'Or

This bustling resort, built around several coves and beaches, is a great spot for water sports. The town looks south to Africa and the low-rise white-washed architecture seems more African than European. A shuttle train (inexpensive) runs between the town centre and marina in summer.

✚ 182 E2

Tourist Information Centre
☎ Cala Llonga, s/n
📞 971 657463
🕐 Mon–Fri 8:30–2

🔟 Cala Figuera

White-painted cottages reach down to the waterfront and fishermen sit on the steps mending their nets at this much-photographed cove, a narrow inlet between the cliffs which is reminiscent

set in a natural harbour on the edge of a wide bay. Porto Colom, which once served as the port for Felanitx, takes its name from the Catalan for Columbus, as this is one of several places which claims to be the birth-place of the explorer Christopher Columbus. The oldest part of the village, behind the harbour, has

Cala Figuera is known as Mallorca's "Little Venice"

of the fjords of Galicia in northwest Spain. Ask before you take photos as some of the fishermen are getting rather tired of having cameras poked in their faces while they are trying to make a living out of diminishing fish stocks. A couple of outdoor cafés overlook the small harbour. The nearest beach is 4km south at Cala Santanyí.

➕ 182 D1

🔟 Salines de Llevant

Located in the southernmost tip of the island are the salt flats of Salines de Llevant. The method is the same age-old one used around the world: sea water is collected in large flat lots or pans, diked by soil, and left in the sun for the moisture to evaporate. The salt which remains takes on a pinkish hue because of the red earth. The surrounding scrub is a habitat for larks, warblers, plovers and stilts.

➕ 182 C2

🔟 Cabrera

This rocky archipelago off the south coast of Mallorca was designated a national park in 1991. It is now protected as one of the last wilderness areas in the Mediterranean, a refuge for seabirds and species such as the Balearic lizard, which has been wiped out on the mainland but survives here. Apart from a few park wardens, Cabrera is uninhabited but it can be visited in summer on an excursion boat from Colònia de Sant Jordi, giving you time to swim, snorkel or follow various walking trails. A steep hike leads up to the castle above the port, once a military barracks and a death-camp for Napoleonic soldiers, while a museum housed in an old wine-cellar describes the history and fragile ecology of this fascinating group of islands.

➕ 182 C1

☎ Boat trips: 971 649034; national park: 971 725010

Ramón Llull

Ramón Llull was the first writer of note in the Catalan language. His statue stands at the foot of the Born in Palma. His left hand holds an open book and his beard is flowing down to the rope belt on his Franciscan robe. Llull was to the manor born in 1235, and had the good fortune to be royally educated alongside the son of Catalan conqueror Jaume I who had wrested Mallorca from the Moors a few years earlier.

Llull married and had two children and seemed destined for a relatively normal life. At the age of 30, however, he did a 180-degree turn, abandoned his family and ran away to the sanctuary at Randa, where he devoted the rest of his life to promoting Christianity. He wrote 100 books in Catalan, his mother tongue, on topics ranging from cuisine to catholicism, and then translated many of them into Latin and Arabic. He also set up a school at Miramar in the Tramuntana to train missionaries. He was consumed by the concept of reason and frenetically and hopelessly tried to explain faith in this way.

Fanatical in his conviction, he sailed to North Africa with the mission of converting Moors to Christianity, but was stoned by infidels. The story goes that his confrères carried him back on board ship to sail back to safe haven in Mallorca, but as his island home appeared on the horizon, he died. He was 80 years old.

Where to... Stay

Prices

Prices are for the least expensive double room in high season, IVA sales tax included. Prices may drop by up to 50 per cent in low season. Breakfast is usually included in the room price. € = under 60 Euros   €€ = 60–120 Euros   €€€ = over 120 Euros

Es Reco de Randa €€€

The word is out on this small, comfortable hotel in the quiet inland village of Randa, so you must book well in advance to secure one of the spacious and luxurious bedrooms decorated in Provençal style. The hotel swimming-pool terrace looks out over the gentle hills. If there's no room at the inn, you can always book for dinner and enjoy the fine food served in the hotel restaurant (▶ 152).

✚ 180 A1 ⊠ Carrer Font 13, Randa
☎ 971 660997; fax: 971 662558;
email: esreco@fehm.es

Monnaber Nou €€€

This delightful old *possessio* nestles into the foothills of the Tramuntana, about a 15-minute drive inland from the bays of Pollença and Alcúdia. This manor house has been lovingly transformed into an exquisite and comfortable hotel, although you may have to get used to waking up to the sound of tinkling sheep bells. There are swimming-pools, tennis-courts and bicycle hire (the Campanet Caves are close by), but it may be hard to tear yourself away from the tranquillity of the hotel terrace. A wonderful buffet breakfast in the dining-room is included in the room price.

✚ 180 A3 ⊠ Predio Monnaber Nou, Campanet ☎ 971 877176; fax: 971 877127; email: info@monnaber.com; www.reisdemallorca.com

Raïms €€

Mallorcan winemaker Javier Oliver and his wife Ana have converted part of their 17th-century manor house in the centre of Algaida into five individually decorated self-catering apartments, each named after a different grape variety. The apartments, some of them housed in the old farm buildings, are set around a peaceful garden of palm and orange trees together with a swimming-pool. Breakfast of Mallorcan specialities is taken in the garden in summer, and cosy log fires are lit in the apartments in winter. The cellar is always open for guests to help themselves to Javier's wine.

✚ 180 A1 ⊠ Carrer Ribera 21, Algaida
☎ 971 665157; fax: 971 665799; email: raims@raims.es; www.raims.es

Read's €€€

This British-owned renovated 16th-century manor house is an easy 15-minute drive from Palma and it is set in the Mallorcan countryside with all its greenery and blossoms. The hotel interior is filled with numerous pieces of original art and all kinds of antiques from furniture to stone statuary to tiny silver boudoir items. One of the four elegant salons features a labour-intensive olive press dating from 1716, reminding you of the luxury of leisure. Modern conveniences include indoor and outdoor pools, Jacuzzi, solarium, sauna and tennis-court. Guest rooms, each different from the other, have direct-dial telephones and satellite TV. The hotel restaurant receives accolades from both diners and critics (▶ 152).

✚ 179 E3 ⊠ Can Moragues, Santa Maria ☎ 971 140261; fax: 971 140762; email: readshotel@readshotel.com; www.readshotel.com

Where to...
Eat and Drink

Prices

The € amount indicates what you can expect to pay per person, for a meal excluding drinks, tax and tip **€** = under 15 Euros **€€** = 15–30 Euros **€€€** = over 30 Euros

Santuari de Sant Salvador €

The monasteries of Mallorca provide an unusual solution to the problem of where to stay if you're on a tight budget. If you have a hire car, you might want a few quiet nights of bright stars here on a hill in this monastery. The daytime view of the plain stretching north to the impressive Tramuntana and of the entire south coast including the island of Cabrera is equally enchanting. Some rooms do have a private bath. The bar/restaurant, marked by the "Ave Maria Purissima" sign, is open from around 9 am until everybody goes to bed. Apart from the grand statue of Christ outside which is almost as imposing as the Christ of the Andes in Rio, it's worth looking in the foyer for the sports shirts, framed with letters from the cycling champion owners giving credit to the Virgin Mary for their victories.

🚩 182 D3 🖂 4km south of Felanitx
☎ 971 827282

Celler Can Amer €€€

This award-winning restaurant began 300 years ago as a bodega for making and maturing wine. The soul of the *celler* today is matriarch Antonia Cantallops who has cooked for hundreds of celebrities, including King Juan Carlos and the president of Spain. Antonia's husband, José Torrens (whose speciality is managing good marriages of wine with food), and their two sons Joan and Bartolomé all work from their own kitchen to create and deliver the best of Balearic cuisine. A de-luxe four-course meal might include fried almond cream, Menorcan lobster with onion, duck breast with olives, and Ibizan cheesecake. The Can Amer wine cellar comprises some 4,000 bottles (about 70 per cent red) from Mallorca and the mainland, selected to complement the food of the islands.

🚩 179 F3 🖂 Carrer Pau 39, Inca
☎ 971 501261 🕙 Mon–Sat 1–4:30, 7:30–midnight

Cal Dimoni €

Algaida is known for its traditional Mallorcan restaurants but this barn of a place on the main road offers a more down-to-earth version of Mallorcan cuisine. A huge fire burns in the corner and waiters dash around with plates of sausages, lamb chops, roast chicken and *pa amb oli* straight off the grill. There are no frills and no accompaniments to the meat unless you order salad and chips. The house wine, served in a rustic jug, goes well with the food and the waiters will bring you a glass of herbal liqueur with your coffee. The name means "house of the devil".

🚩 180 A1 🖂 Carretera Palma–Manacor, Km 21, Algaida ☎ 971 665035 🕙 Thu–Tue noon–midnight

Can Pep Noguera €€

Why have lunch in a banana plantation? Because it is there, even though it doesn't seem like Mallorca. The fresh seafood and barbecued lamb are always good, and the service efficient and elegant, in spite of the fact that children are welcome to wander. If you miss passing this way at a mealtime, you can always have a coffee in the bar with the fireplace at the end, after you tour the exotic and intriguing tropical gardens and animal farm.

➕ **182 E3** ⊠ **Carretera Porto Colom–Porto Cristo, Km 4.5, S'Espinagar** ☎ **971 833355** 🕒 **Tue–Sun 1–4, 7–midnight**

Es Reco de Randa €€€

Located in the quiet village of Randa away from the hustle and bustle of coastal resorts, Es Reco is hidden away in the hotel of the same name (▶ 150). The pork liver pâté with almonds and hazelnuts as an appetiser, followed by aubergine stuffed with cod, make a flavourful, complete meal. Service is first class. A common complaint is that the waiters are sometimes slow to bring the bill, but that's a Spanish custom. Es Reco belongs to the Chaîne des Rotisseurs.

➕ **180 A1** ⊠ **Carrer Font 13, Randa** ☎ **971 660997; fax: 971 662558; email: esreco@fehm.es** 🕒 **Daily 12:30–4, 7:30–11:30**

Monnaber Nou €€€

This is deluxe dining at its best: an old Mallorcan estate restored to past glory and elegance (▶ 150). The dining-room overlooks fields of sheep grazing under olive and carob trees. The little lamb chops grilled with cloves of garlic are as crisp and tender as they ought to be and the lamb stuffed with spinach is divine. Or try the rabbit with onions tinged with a touch of tomato and cinnamon, a Mallorcan classic. Both the almond cake and the lemon mousse, made from local zesty lemons, make a tasty dessert. Staff are friendly and the service is superior.

➕ **180 A3** ⊠ **4km from Campanet** ☎ **971 877176** 🕒 **Daily 1–3:30, 7:30–11**

Read's €€€

If you want to really dress up and go out for dinner, here's a prizewinning restaurant to try. The British chef Marc Fosh was recently awarded his first Michelin star. Allow extra time, both to browse around the artwork and antiques of the hotel salons, and to plough through the elaborate menu descriptions. Typical appetisers include: pan-fried *foie gras* with black pudding tempura, apple and sage purée and a cabernet *jus*; and *sashimi* of salmon and fresh tuna marinated in soy sauce with guacamole and coriander oil. Main courses include: John Dory with pea ravioli, asparagus and sauce brandade; and roasted filet of lamb with couscous and a bitter orange and thyme *jus*.

Dessert combos vary from caramelised apple lasagne with ginger ice-cream and passion fruit caramel sauce to crispy orange and sesame *tuilles* with a coconut sorbet and a minestrone of fresh fruits. Meanwhile, a life-size painting of Bacchus looks down from a *trompel'oeil* window on the wall.

➕ **179 E3** ⊠ **Can Moragues, Santa Maria** ☎ **971 14026l; fax: 971 140762; email: readshotel@readshotel.com;**

www.readshotel.com 🕒 **Daily 1–3.30, 7:30–11**

Sa Creu €€

This is the place for a delicious meal at a bargain price. The threecourse *menu del dia* (€) will leave you wanting to siesta the afternoon away. Tables are set with a basket of bread, a bowl of tart green olives and a bottle of wine from neighbouring vineyards. There is always a choice of dishes. The first course is usually a tureen of bold fish or meat broth with rice or pasta. If you eat the whole thing, there will be little space left for the main course of rabbit with onion, veal cutlet or hake with chips. The fresh fruit salad for dessert is hard to match anywhere. Cap the meal with a *café cortado*, an espresso with a dash of milk, especially if you're driving. The *cortado* costs extra. On Sundays, families come here for the surrounding area come here for the big midday meal. Occasionally Sa Creu is closed to the public for a wedding, baptism or communion celebration and feast.

➕ 180 C2 ⌧ Carretera Manacor–Inca, Km 9, Petra ☎ 971 830246 ◉ Mon–Thu 7 am–8 pm, Fri–Sun 7 am–11 pm

Ses Canyes €€

This is one of those rare restaurants that Mallorcans have managed to keep for themselves – until now. You could almost make a meal of the country-style bread, black olives and the robust red table wine, all pleasantly delivered by black-waist-coated waiters, but leave room for the suckling pig or the spring lamb shoulder grilled over a wood fire. Yes, you can use your hands to eat every scrap of the meat. Drapes in the typical Mallorcan tongues pattern frame the windows and original oil landscapes adorn the walls, while ceiling fans overhead lend a tropical air.

➕ 180 A1 ⌧ Carretera Manacor, Km 15.2, Algaida ☎ 971 742498 ◉ Daily 8:30 am–11 pm

Where to...
Shop

Antiques

The Sunday morning (9–2) *rastrillo* in Consell brings out some of the best treasures and worst junk on the island. The earlier the hour the better the bargains, and the later the hour the bigger the crowds. Some vendors are professionals who continually buy and sell for profit, while others are simply Mallorcans and expatriates lightening their load. Most vendors are friendly, and prices are negotiable.

Glass

Vidrieria Gordiola (Carretera Palma-Manacor, Km 19) is the oldest glass-blowing enterprise on the island. You can watch artisans blow the molten crystal and roll it into oil and vinegar jugs, coloured vases, candlesticks, candelabras and even elaborate chandeliers. Other glass companies are **Lafiore** (Km 11 on the Palma–Valldemossa road) and **Menestralia** (Km 36 on the Palma–Alcudia road).

Leather

While nearly every urban centre has shops selling quality leather goods, Inca has been the undisputed leather capital of the island since the mid-1800s. Leather shops line the main road and several city streets; some have expanded into ware-houses, cafés and restaurants. You can enjoy traditional Mallorcan foods at Anthony's Restaurant, while you ponder a purchase at **Anthony's Leather Factory & Shop** adjacent (just behind the filling station on the turn-off to Sineu from the main road through Inca, tel: 971 504266). A raft of nearby stores with names like **Albaladejo**, **Asinca**, **Munper**, **Pelinca** and **Yanko** also offer a vast variety of leather goods. The Albaladejo family, who have been shoemakers for a century, produce only for their own shops and offer quality designs. Genuine bargains are available, but it takes ferreting around to find them.

Markets

Apart from the Wednesday morning market in Sineu, one of the best (▶ 144), most inland and southern towns have weekly outdoor markets. Prices are sometimes lower in less touristy areas.

Pearls

It's a toss-up between **Perlas Majórica** (Av Majórica 48, Manacor) and **Perlas Orquidea** (Montuiri) both creators of manufactured pearls. You can tour either factory for a glimpse of how these pearls are made, although the actual recipe is a long-guarded secret. Both factories, as well as most souvenir shops around the island, sell Mallorcan pearls plain or made into pins, pendants, necklaces, bracelets, earrings and rings.

Wine

If you're staying a while, or can figure out how to take a case home with you, visit the **Bodegues Oliver** (tel: 971 561117) in Petra, a few streets from the Serra Museum. Their red wines vary from very good to excellent and are exceptionally good quality for the price. Table wine by the bottle is usually cheaper in small grocery shops inland.

Shopping Centres

Festival Park (tel: 971 140925; www.festivalparks.com) is a major new shopping and leisure centre which opened in 2002 just off the Palma to Inca motorway at Marratxi. The complex comprises factory outlets, designer shops, a craft market, restaurants and bars, children's play areas, a bowling alley and a reptile house for the kids. Among the other attractions is a 20-screen multiplex cinema which shows original versions of English-language blockbusters soon after their release.

Where to...
Be Entertained

The preferred Mallorcan evening-out entertainment is an elaborate meal with friends in a restaurant, at home or in a countryside *finca*. You won't find much urban-style nightlife inland, and little more in south-coast resorts.

Horse-riding

Horse-riding has been a popular Spanish sport from earliest times. Many local horses are of superior Arab stock. Assuming you've got an amiable steed, there is no better way to enjoy the pastoral peace of inland country trails; you can ride like Don Quixote among the old windmills. Numerous agrotourism guest ranches have horses for riding. Several other establishments offer lessons in riding (English, Andalusian or Western), jumping and dressage, as well as guided excursions into the surrounding countryside. You are normally required to take a lesson before you head out, just to make sure there will be no problems on the trail.

Horse-trotting

Horse-trotting is a popular spectator sport, in which the jockey sits in a small cart behind the horse and has to prevent the horse from breaking into a gallop. The sport has been popular in Mallorca for at least 200 years, and friends and family will often go out together for a day at the races. Most people have a small bet on the horses. Trotting races take place every Saturday at the hippodrome in Manacor (Carretera Palma–Arta, Km 50; tel: 971 550023), at 9 pm from June to October and at 4 pm the rest of the year. You can also see trotting races at Son Pardo hippodrome, just outside Palma on the road to Soller (tel: 971 754031), at 9 pm on Friday evenings in July and August and at 4 pm on Sunday afternoons for the rest of the year.

Stargazing

Here in the dark of night when the towns have gone to sleep, the stars seem closer than almost anywhere else in the world. Contact the observatory in Costitx for a closer look: Observatorio Astronómico de Mallorca (tel: 971 876019; Coxtitx–Sencelles road, Km 1).

Resort Sports

South-coast beach resorts offer such holiday diversions as swimming, snorkelling, scuba-diving, sailing, windsurfing, tennis, cycling, walking and hiking.

Walks

1 PUIG MARIA

Walk

DISTANCE About 4km **TIME** 1.5 hours, plus an hour or so for lunch and for looking around

START POINT Km 52 on the main Pollença–Palma road (PM-220) 🗺 180 B4
END POINT As above ☎ 971 184132 (Monastery and restaurant)

Puig (pronounced "pooch") Maria is one of Pollença's most sacred shrines and is a popular pilgrimage site for both Mallorcans and visitors. Many Pollençines make the trek up to the shrine every Easter Monday to give thanks for life's blessings. Some people come for religious reasons. Others come for the walk, for the air, for the views, and some simply come for lunch.

1–2

Leave your car in Pollença, make your way out to the main road, cross carefully and look for a minor lane on the far side, signposted "Puig de Maria". This is the start of the walk. The limestone sugar loaf ahead looms straight up 380m. On either side lie farm fields with goats and sheep, and fig and carob trees. Follow the lane as it meanders back and forth past several farms and country homes. Beyond the last

house (with black metal gates), the narrow concreted road zigzags upwards.

2–3

As you climb, there are occasional glimpses through the trees to the red tile roofs capping the ochre and white buildings of Pollença.

POLLENÇA

← Palma

PM-220

Pines and oaks along the trail offer shade from the hot sun

Page 155: La Reserva gives you a taste of the Serra Tramuntana

To the northwest, ridges of mountains soar upwards towards the sky. Clear skies may even present a glimpse of the white communications spheres which look like two gigantic golf-balls crowning Puig Major, the island's highest peak. (1,445m). As the trail rises, holm oaks give way to Aleppo pines. Note the intriguing patterns in shades of terracotta and ochre on the pine bark.

The "Sanctuary in the Sky" welcomes visitors of all faiths

3–4

The lane gradually shifts around to the western face of the mountain, providing splendid views of the Vall de Colonya and Mount Axartell (440m) beyond. The main road below runs from Pollença to Palma. In front of the south side of the mountain lies the Pollença Golf Club mostly hidden from view. If you look closely, however, you catch a glimpse of one of the greens.

4–5

After a steep scenic turn, on the north side of the road is a parking spot for two cars, reserved for the couple who take care of the monastery now that all the monks and nuns have left. Behind, there is a cave, but be wary: hidden dark chutes fall into the middle of the mountain. The road now turns into the Pilgrims' Stairs, broad steps of stones leading up the trail. Just after the second switchback, on the right you will see Cradle Rock, a cross-marked natural rock seat beside a small cave where barren couples traditionally pray for children. After several more switchbacks, the Puig Maria peeks through the pine trees and mata bushes.

5

Inside the castellated courtyard stands the Gothic defence tower, rebuilt several times since the 15th century. Behind the tower and past the picnic tables and barbecue grills, lies the panorama of Pollença Bay backdropped by the Formentor peninsula and the blue Mediterranean. Southeast stands Alcúdia town, port, peninsula and its broad bay sweeping southwards.

The chapel was originally built in 1348 probably to honour the Virgin Mary for ending the Great Plague. Local legend tells of three hermitesses who lived on a neighbouring mountain about that time and who saw lights on Puig Maria one night. They walked up, found an image of the Virgin, and, as a result, built a hermitage there. Whatever its history, candles are always lit. By the 16th century, monks had taken over, but they were obliged to abandon the monastery when the Council of Trent ordered them to live closer to their flocks. Later, nuns lived here for many years, but the last nun left in 1988. Since then, management has been in private hands. Walk behind the altar from right to left to see the statue of the Virgin and Child (who is playing with a little hawk), which is brought down to the town once every 50 years (the next time is in 2049!). Dark paintings decorate the walls and glass cases in the main entrance hall protect ancient pottery. The best treasures have been moved to the museum in Pollença for safe keeping. Regular services are held in the Puig Maria chapel every Sunday and on special occasions throughout the year.

Lunch is not served in the 15th-century refectory with its long tables and well at one end. Instead, climb up the stairs to the counter in the main hall, and ring the hanging bell.

restaurant is closed on Mondays. Let the waiter know if you want to buy souvenirs from the shop. Or maybe you'll want to rent one of the cheap spartan rooms with a million-dollar view and stay the night (to reserve a room in advance, tel: 971 184132).

Otherwise, gently retrace your steps down the mountain.

The monastery enjoys spectacular views in all directions

Hiking Hints

Even the winter sun can be hot. Carry a hat, sunscreen, sunglasses and a bottle of water. An umbrella can protect you from both excessive rain and sun. Walking shoes with good grip are best, especially for slippery rock or gravel.

Let someone know where you're going and when you'll be back or, better still, join a group walk if you can. A mobile phone could be a lifesaver in the event of an emergency. Leave gates closed or open as you find them, and leave flowers and plants for others to enjoy too.

Stay on the trail, unless you know the area well or have an experienced guide – some slopes hide unmarked holes and caves.

Someone will surface to take your order and will bring it to the small dining-room adjacent. The food and wine are good and reasonably priced. Try the paella or *arros brut* for a hot meal. For a sandwich, it's hard to beat the *pa amb oli*. The

2 BÓQUER VALLEY

Walk

DISTANCE About 6km **TIME** About 2 hours plus picnic time
START POINT Port de Pollença, Avinguda Bocchoris: Km 0.6 on the PM-221 road to Formentor
END POINT As above
180 B5

The Bóquer Valley is beautiful and accessible, running roughly from one Mediterranean shore to another, across the eastern edge of the Tramuntana range. Wild goats graze on rosemary and other green plants growing high among the craggy rocks. Birds migrate through this valley, especially during April and October.

1–2
The walk begins on Avinguda Bocchoris, a broad avenue of pine and tamarisk trees leading to the Bóquer farm. You can get there from the centre of Port de Pollença by following the "Pine Walk" north from the fishing harbour with the sea on your right. When the promenade narrows, continue to the end of the first section of beach and look

for Avinguda Bocchoris on your left. Cross the main road and walk uphill on a clearly marked path to the big green gates of the farmhouse.

2–3
Go through the gate and up the drive-way to the front of the old farmhouse, still sporting a defence tower from the 17th century. Look back down to the plain for a panoramic view of Pollença Bay and the road running west to Pollença and beyond into the Lluc Valley.

3–4
Continue past the farmhouse and through a metal gate. Follow the stony track a few metres to the right to climb to another gate.

4–5
Now you are in the Bóquer Valley. The broad stony trail steadily climbs along the right-hand side of the valley. To the left, the 360-m high limestone ridge, Cavall Bernat, runs north to

Clumps of pistachia and rosemary line the relatively flat trail

the sea, divided here and there by rock walls climbing from the valley floor up to the sky.

5–6

The first markers along the trail are the 15-m high rock outcrops towering overhead. Head left for a few metres, through the clumps of the *garballo* (dwarf palm) native to this part of Mallorca. Hidden at the base of a huge boulder is a small cave for shelter from winter wind and rain. The mouth of the cave has been partly stoned in at some time in the past, probably to contain sheep and goats.

Private property

It would be easy to be put off by the forbidding notices on the gates of the Bóquer farmhouse reminding walkers that you are entering private land. The growing popularity of walking in Mallorca in recent years has led many landowners to attempt to deny access. The legal position is that you are fully entitled to follow this walk, but you must stay on the footpath and respect the rights of the property owner. As this is a working farm, that means in particular not disturbing livestock, not allowing dogs on this walk and not leaving any litter behind.

Downhill from here, the trail dips and broadens into a wide dirt path.

6–7

To the left just past the gap in a limestone wall, is a long-abandoned stone kiln, used years ago to fire limestone to produce lime and whitewash. The lime pit is about 4m deep and 3m in diameter. At one time, lime was used as a disinfectant, and before paint took over, it used to be the custom in Spain to whitewash houses every

spring. West across the valley, a stone wall runs up the mountainside. Look closely and you will see several piles of stones, south of the wall near the bottom of the slope. These are the 2,500-year-old remnants of the walls of the old Talaiot town of Bocchoris, where the oblong stone houses were flat on one end and rounded on the other like boats. Shortly after the Romans arrived in 123 BC, Bóquer confederated with Rome and the community faded within a few generations.

7–8

The trail now climbs up to a plateau with an umbrella pine grove, a shady spot for refreshments. In springtime, wild cyclamen and orchids blossom in this area, and you may also disturb the occasional wild goat.

Punta Troneta

Cala Bóquer

355m

Serra del Cavall Bernat

Coll del Moro

fishermen's shelter

9

10

8

pine grove

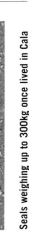

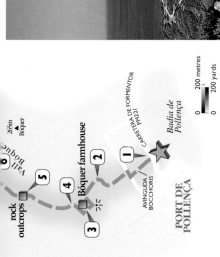

200 metres
200 yards

CARRETERA DE FORMENTOR
CARRETERA PM21

Badia de Pollença

AVINGUDA / BOCCHORIS

PORT DE POLLENÇA

rock outcrops

Vall Bóque[r]

265m ▲ Bóquer

5

4

Bóquer farmhouse

3

2

1

Seals weighing up to 300kg once lived in Cala Bóquer. They are now being reintroduced.

8–9

Your route meanders gently upwards from the pine grove and through another old stone wall towards the Coll del Moro (Moor's Hill) at 80m.

The main path now heads downto the sea, then several small paths run off to the left and down to the stony beach. Stay on the path which swings to the right and winds through clumps of palm and rosemary to a grassy knoll and a rocky outcrop overlooking Cala Bóquer. Now you are at one of the most picturesque picnic spots on the island. To the east, limestone ridges rise from the sea almost straight up to the sky. Beyond, just offshore, stands the rocky island of Es Colomer. The Serra Cavall Bernat shelters the little cove from the mistral, the strong northwest wind that sometimes sweeps in from France.

9–10

You may want to wander down to the beach and the fishermen's shelter. Although the beach is rather gravelly and littered with small flotsam and jetsam, the snorkelling is excellent.

To return to Port de Pollença, simply retrace your route. The views on the way back are equally dramatic, yet different enough to

make this route seem like quite another walk. If you still have some energy left when you return, turn left along the seafront to follow the pine-shaded promenade to its end.

Top tip

• There's little shade in this valley. Carry drinking water and wear a hat to guard against the Spanish sun.

3 TRAMUNTANA Son Marroig

Walk

This route leads down to Sa Foradada, a romantic peninsula of pines ending in a barren rock outcrop with an 18-m wide hole through it. It's a prominent landmark for sailors and landlubbers alike along the Tramuntana coast.

DISTANCE 6km return **TIME** 2 hours plus lunch and/or swim time
START POINT Son Marroig, located at Km 66 on the C-710 road between Valldemossa and Deià. Park in the car-park in front of the house ✚ 179 D4
END POINT As above ☎ 971 639158 (Museum and house)

1–2

Before you set out on the walk, stop at the Son Marroig manor house (▶ 101) to buy a ticket (inexpens ve) because the trail is on private land . The classical belvedere in the garden offers a clear view of the rock, your destination. Leaving the house, turn right along a lane and look out for a gate on your right, marked "'No Pasar Sin Autorización". Scramble over the rungs of the stile to the

right of the gate. This broad bridle-path, built a century ago by Austrian ecologist Archduke Luis Salvador who bought Son Marroig in 1870, forks about 100m along.

2–3

Take the right-hand trail, which snakes back and forth down the mountainside. After the first few curves, you will see a cliff above your head eroded to form shallow caves, with

Punta Prima

Restaurant

5 boat landing

Punta de sa Foradada

6 Cova des Xaloc

big hole

The defence tower of the manor house was built as a lookout for pirates

3–4

When you reach sea level, the trail splits again. To the left, the trail deteriorates but follows the sea along to S'Estaca, once a Sicilian-style farm where the Archduke romanced Catalina Homer, the daughter of a local carpenter. S'Estaca is now owned by American actor Michael Douglas. Keep on the main path which bears right and skirts the wooded peninsula. From here you can see the sweep of the coastline north to Punta de Deià. The path soon curves left to a small land-bridge leading to the rocky promontory.

4–5

Bear right and drop down to the left to a small boat-landing, where the Archduke used to moor his grand yacht, *Nixe*. This is a fine place for a picnic or a swim or both. Alternatively, the left-hand track climbs to a small white building, a restaurant open in summer to cater for hikers and visitors sailing in on the Port de Sóller

stalactites draping down in front.

About half-way down to the sea, on your left, a flight of steep stone steps leads up to a round platform, a pleasant place to stop and rest and look out to the pierced rock. If the sea is rough, you may hear a loud bellowing, sounding like a cross between a whale and chainsaw, as the waves wash the caves in the rocks.

As the trail descends to the sea, the screeching of gulls and cormorants is a constant chorus

Pirate Cruise. Here also you may want to relax with a coffee and write some postcards.

To return to Son Marroig, retrace your steps back up the mountainside.

6
Adventure Option (allow an additional hour)

Climb carefully up the rocky slope, and slowly make your way out to the land-bridge across the huge l'ole in the rock. On three sides, the rock plunges straight down to the sea 80m below. The view southwest along the coast to Sa Dragonera Island, a nature reserve which marks the western tip of the Tramuntana, is equally dramatic. To the northeast, beyond Punta de Deià looms Puig Major. Southwest stands Puig Carago'i, where another of the Archduke's bridle-paths, still in good shape a century later, leads up to and around this peak. Down a little to the right is the Archduke's mountain refuge hut. Please note that this option involves some scrambling and is for experienced climbers only.

According to Archduke Luis Salvador, the best way to savour the area's wild splendour is to sail around Sa Foradada into the sunset

4 S'ALBUFERA
Bird-watching

Walk

DISTANCE 2–5km **TIME** 1–2 hours
START POINT 5km south from Port d'Alcúdia on the main C-712 road to Artà ⊞ 180 C4
END POINT As above ☎ 971 892250; fax: 971 892158; www.mallorcaweb.net/salbufera/
⊙ Daily 9–7, Apr–Sep; 9–5, rest of year ⊠ Free, but registration requested

In 1988 S'Albufera wetland, became the first protected nature park in the Balearics. These 800ha have been developing and improving under the watchful eyes of local biologists. The name comes from the Arabic and means "lagoon". The last industry working in the swamp, making paper from reeds and sedges, closed in 1966.

1–2

A canal separating the Alcúdia and Muro beaches links the S'Albufera swamp to the sea. Watch for the big Parc Natural Hotel on the east side of the road and the narrow bridge over the Gran Canal. Just south of the bridge, a gated country lane runs off westwards. This is the park entrance. Just south of the country lane is a parking area for S'Albufera visitors.

The S'Albufera wetland was formed 100,000 years ago, but the sea dunes are far younger

2–3

Follow the country lane for 1km to the Sa Roca Reception Office to register. Pick up a map of the park and a list of birds sighted within the past fortnight: there is space to record your sightings.

Top tips Bird-watching is best in spring and autumn, when migrating species stop here for feeding and fresh water on their journeys north and south. The best times of day are sunrise and sunset. Be sure to bring mosquito repellent.

• One of the best ways to see the wetlands is by bicycle. There is a cycle hire shop on the west side of the C-712 road, about a kilometre north of the park entrance. The Parc Natural Hotel can also arrange cycle hire.

In the 17th century local farmers created small fields, surrounding them with canals – thus creating an effective irrigation system.

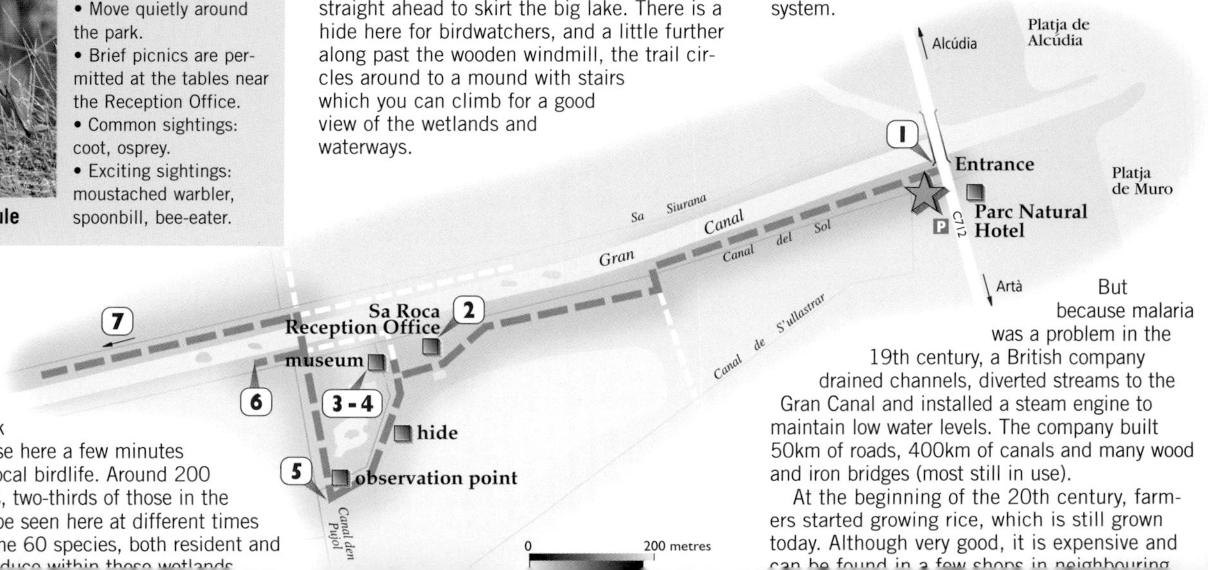

4–5

Trails are well marked and there is little danger of getting lost. Leaving the museum, turn right outside the door, cross the road and keep straight ahead to skirt the big lake. There is a hide here for birdwatchers, and a little further along past the wooden windmill, the trail circles around to a mound with stairs which you can climb for a good view of the wetlands and waterways.

But because malaria was a problem in the 19th century, a British company drained channels, diverted streams to the Gran Canal and installed a steam engine to maintain low water levels. The company built 50km of roads, 400km of canals and many wood and iron bridges (most still in use).

At the beginning of the 20th century, farmers started growing rice, which is still grown today. Although very good, it is expensive and can be found in a few shops in neighbouring

Birds Are Beautiful
- Respect the birds and their habitat.
- Move quietly around the park.
- Brief picnics are permitted at the tables near the Reception Office.
- Common sightings: coot, osprey.
- Exciting sightings: moustached warbler, spoonbill, bee-eater.

Purple gallinule

3–4
Straight ahead 50m is the park museum. Browse here a few minutes for an idea of local birdlife. Around 200 species of birds, two-thirds of those in the Balearics, can be seen here at different times of the year. Some 60 species, both resident and migratory, reproduce within these wetlands

Map labels: Alcúdia, Platja de Alcúdia, Platja de Muro, Entrance, Parc Natural Hotel, Artà, C712, P, Sa Siurana, Canal del Sol, Gran Canal, Canal de S'Illot, Reception Office, Sa Roca, museum, hide, observation point, Canal den Pujol, 0 200 metres

1, 2, 3–4, 5, 6, 7

Flora Is Fun

● The most exciting swamp flower is the bright spring-blooming lax-flowered orchid, which grows to almost 1m in open areas beside reed beds.

● Most of the marsh is covered with a dense mass of reeds and sedges. Reedmace grows in the channels, while yellow-crees, duckweed and hornwort prefer the quieter waters. Elms and white poplars flourish along the dyke trails, providing leafy shade in summer.

● On the coastal sand dunes where salinity increases, tamarisk, pine and juniper grow. Glasswort grows where the soil dries up in summer.

Above: Wild rosemary grows all over the island

Tant towns. In the 1960s, tourism developers transformed large tracts of the marsh into building sites for houses, apartments, hotels and the restaurants, bars and other services that accompany them.

5–6

Continue on this path as it bends round to the right, passing the Sa Roca maintenance buildings. On the right in a small pond, you may see the purple gallinule, prized as a banquet feast by the Romans 2,000 years ago. Straight ahead, just before the bridge that crosses the Gran Canal, turn left and walk to the gated pasture at the end, passing a bird-watching hide on the right.

6–7

Go back to the bridge and walk across. From the bridge you have good views of the Gran Canal east and west, and of the ducks and other fowl feeding therein. After the bridge, turn left and continue straight ahead. This long trail leads to several hides where you can while away the day.

Retrace your route back to the Reception Office, the road and your vehicle.

The swamp attracts wildlife of all kinds

5 TRAMUNTANA
La Reserva
Walk

DISTANCE About 4km **TIME** About 2 hours plus picnic time
START POINT La Reserva car-park, 19km northwest of Palma, via Puigpunyent ✚ 178 C2
END POINT As above ☺ Daily 10–sunset ☎ 971 616622 (Park office)

La Reserva is a natural paradise, improved by people for people. Stone stairways make getting up and down the slopes easier, there are descriptive signs in Catalan, Spanish, English and German at almost every turn and green arrows mark the route.

Clinging to the southeastern skirt of Galatzo, Mallorca's most mystical mountain (1,026m), La Reserva's 200,000sq m of lush wilderness include 3km of easy walking trails, dozens of waterfalls and several caves. Galatzo is so magnetic that many pilots avoid flying over it for fear of losing control of their planes.

Buy a ticket (moderate) at the entrance, then head along the winding trail to the Mirador de la Reina (the Queen's Lookout) for a vista of Es Ratxo Valley where Mallorca's first known residents lived 8,000 years ago.

Follow the route to the right past an impressive waterfall to the Coves Negres (Black Caves) which have been hollowed out by the water.

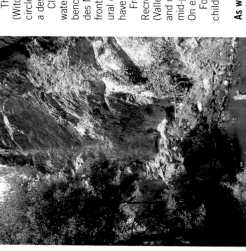

The next stop is Recó de ses Bruixes (Witches' Remembrance) with a charcoal kiln circle and a charcoal-maker's cave hut. There is a description of the charcoal-making process.

Climb back uphill past the rock which exudes water, and the rest area (with a sun-shelter, benches and a cold-drink machine), to the Cova des Moro (Moor's Cave) with a peaceful pond in front. From this viewpoint you can see the natural defences on the summit of Es Ratxo which have been used since prehistoric times.

From the Moor's Cave, it's a short walk to the Recreation Area. The Vall de les Sis Fonts (Valley of the Six Springs), with toilets, a bar and café and a barbecue/picnic area, is the mid-point and the best place to stop and rest. On exhibit are owls, falcons and other birds. Follow the green arrows to the exit, the children's playground, and back to the car-park.

As well as dozens of waterfalls, La Reserva harbours a variety of indigenous plants

Websites
- Spanish Tourist Board·
  www.tourspain.es
- Balearic Islands:
  www.visitbalears.com

In Mallorca
- Palma Tourist Office
  Plaça de la Reina 2
  Palma 07001
  ☎ 971 712216

- Mallorca Tourist Board
  Fomento del Turismo
  de Mallorca, Carrer de
  Constitució, 1, Palma
  ☎ 971 725396

BEFORE YOU GO

WHAT YOU NEED

- ● Required
- ○ Suggested
- ▲ Not required
- △ Not applicable

	UK	Germany	USA	Canada	Australia	Ireland	Netherlands	Spain
Passport/National Identity Card	●	●	●	●	●	●	●	△
Visa	▲	▲	▲	▲	▲	▲	▲	▲
Onward or Return Ticket	○	○	●	●	●	○	○	○
Health Inoculations (tetanus and polio)	▲	▲	▲	▲	▲	▲	▲	▲
Health Documentation (►174, Health)	●	●	▲	▲	▲	●	●	▲
Travel Insurance	○	○	○	○	○	○	○	○
Driving Licence (national)	●	●	●	●	●	●	●	●
Car Insurance Certificate	●	●	●	●	●	●	●	○
Car Registration Document	●	●	●	●	●	●	●	○

WHEN TO GO

Palma

▭ High season   ▭ Low season

JAN	FEB	MAR	APR	MAY	JUN	JUL	AUG	SEP	OCT	NOV	DEC
14°C	15°C	17°C	19°C	22°C	26°C	29°C	29°C	27°C	23°C	18°C	15°C

☀ Sun   ☁ Cloud   🌧 Wet   🌦 Sun/Showers

The temperatures displayed above are the average daily maximum for each
month. Minimum temperatures are considerably lower than this, sometimes drop-
ping to 2 or 3°C in January and February but rarely falling below 20°C in July and
August. There is almost guaranteed sunshine throughout the summer months,
the peak tourist season. For mild, pleasant weather but to avoid the worst of the
crowds, the best months are May, June, September and October. Many of the
resorts and tourist facilities close down in winter, though this is a good time for a
walking or golfing holiday or a city break in Palma. Even in winter it is usually
warm enough to eat lunch out of doors, though you will need a sweater and jacket
for cool winter evenings, especially in the mountains.

In the UK
● Spanish Tourist Office
22–3 Manchester Square
London
W1M 5AP
☎ 020 7486 8077

In the US
● Tourist Office of Spain
666 Fifth Ave (35th Floor)
New York
NY 10103
☎ 212 265 8822

In the US
● Tourist Office of Spain
1221 Brickell Ave
Miami
FL 33131
☎ 305 358 1992

GETTING THERE

By Air Palma's Son Sant Joan Airport (tel: 971 789099) is one of the busiest in Europe in summer, with up to 800 flights arriving each day. The Spanish national airline, Iberia, has regular flights from Madrid, Barcelona and other Spanish cities.

From the UK British Airways flies from London Gatwick and British Midland from London Heathrow to Palma. Other options include easyJet from Bristol, Gatwick, Liverpool, Luton and Stansted, and Air Scotland from Edinburgh and Glasgow. There are numerous charter flights to Mallorca from regional UK airports, especially in summer. Most seats are sold through tour operators as part of a package holiday, but you can pick up a flight-only deal through travel agents or on the internet (for example, www.cheapflights.com).

From the rest of Europe Iberia flies to Palma from most major European cities, though you will need to change planes in Barcelona or Madrid. There are also direct charter flights from regional airports in Germany, Ireland and elsewhere.

From the US There are no direct flights from the US to Mallorca, though Iberia flies from New York, Los Angeles and Miami via Madrid or Barcelona.

From Australia and New Zealand There are no direct flights to Spain, so the cheapest and easiest method is to fly to London and pick up a connection from there.

By boat There are regular ferry services connecting Palma to Barcelona and Valencia on the Spanish mainland as well as to the Balearic islands of Menorca and Ibiza.

TIME

 Like the rest of Spain, Mallorca is one hour ahead of Greenwich Mean Time (GMT+1), with summer time (GMT+2) in operation from the last Sunday in March to the last Sunday in October. The Spanish attitude to time is more laid-back than in northern Europe and everything happens very late. Mealtimes are typically 1–4 pm for lunch and 9 pm–midnight for dinner, though restaurants in the main tourist resorts have largely adapted to northern European hours. Night-clubs and discos start around midnight and go on until morning.

CURRENCY AND FOREIGN EXCHANGE

Currency The official currency of Spain is the Euro, issued in notes of 5, 10, 20, 50, 100, 200 and 500 Euros and in coins of 1 and 2 Euros as well as 1, 2, 5, 10, 20 and 50 cents. Euro notes are identical throughout all countries in the Eurozone; the coins have national symbols on one side but are equally accepted everywhere. Euros are also legal tender in many other European countries, including France, Germany, Ireland, Italy and Portugal. The major international credit cards are widely accepted in Mallorca. Spain's previous currency, the peseta, was abolished in 2002.

Exchange Banks generally offer the best rates for changing foreign currency and travellers' cheques, though money can also be changed at many travel agents, exchange bureaux and hotels. You will need to show your passport when changing travellers' cheques. You can also withdraw cash from cashpoint machines using your credit or debit card and a PIN (personal identification number), though your bank will usually make a charge for this service.

TIME DIFFERENCES

GMT	Mallorca	USA New York	Germany	Rest of Spain	Australia
12 noon	→ 1 pm	← 7 am	→ 1 pm	→ 1 pm	→ Sydney 10 pm

WHEN YOU ARE THERE

CLOTHING SIZES

UK	Rest of Europe	USA	
36	46	36	
38	48	38	
40	50	40	
42	52	42	Suits
44	54	44	
46	56	46	
7	41	8	
7.5	42	8.5	
8.5	43	9.5	
9.5	44	10.5	Shoes
10.5	45	11.5	
11	46	12	
14.5	37	14.5	
15	38	15	
15.5	39/40	15.5	
16	41	16	Shirts
16.5	42	16.5	
17	43	17	
8	34	6	
10	36	8	
12	38	10	
14	40	12	Dresses
16	42	14	
18	44	16	
4.5	38	6	
5	38	6.5	
5.5	39	7	
6	39	7.5	
6.5	40	8	Shoes
7	41	8.5	

NATIONAL HOLIDAYS

1 Jan	New Year's Day
6 Jan	Epiphany
Mar/Apr	Good Friday, Easter Monday
1 May	Labour Day
15 Aug	Assumption of the Virgin
12 Oct	National Day
1 Nov	All Saints' Day
6 Dec	Constitution Day
8 Dec	Feast of the Immaculate Conception
25 Dec	Christmas Day

Many shops and offices close for longer periods around Christmas and Easter, as well as for the festivals of Corpus Christi in May/June and Sant Jaume on 25 July.

OPENING HOURS

○ Shops ● Offices ● Banks
● Post Offices ● Museums/Monuments ● Pharmacies

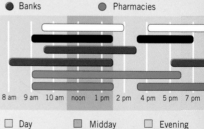

8 am   9 am   10 am   noon   1 pm   2 pm   4 pm   5 pm   7 pm

□ Day   ■ Midday   □ Evening

In addition to the times shown above, large department stores, supermarkets and shops in resorts may open outside these times, especially in summer. In general, pharmacies, banks and shops close on Saturday afternoon, though banks stay open until 4:30 pm Monday to Thursday, October to May, but close Saturday, June to September. The opening times of museums is a rough guide; some are open longer hours in summer. Some museums close at weekends or a day in the week.

POLICE (POLICÍA NACIONAL) 112

FIRE (BOMBEROS) 112

AMBULANCE (AMBULÀNCIA) 112

PERSONAL SAFETY

The national police force, the Policía Nacional (brown uniforms) keep law and order in urban areas. Some resorts have their own tourist-friendly Policía Turística. If you need a police station ask for *la comisaría*.

To help prevent crime:

- Do not carry more cash than you need.
- Do not leave valuables on the beach or poolside.
- Beware of pickpockets in markets, tourist sights or crowded places.
- Avoid walking alone in dark alleys at night.

Police assistance:

☎ **112** from any phone

TELEPHONES

Public telephones have instructions in several languages. Most take coins, credit cards or phonecards (*tarjetas telefónicas*) which are available from post offices, kiosks and tobacconists.

All telephone numbers in the Balearic Islands begin with 971; this is part of the phone number, so you must dial all nine digits wherever you are calling from. To call the operator dial 002.

International Dialling Codes

From Mallorca (Spain) to

UK:	00 44
USA:	00 1
Ireland:	00 353
Australia:	00 61
Germany:	00 49
Netherlands:	00 31
Spain:	00 34

POST

Post offices (*correus*) are open as shown on page 172 but some also open in the afternoon and on Saturday morning. The main post office in Palma at Carrer de Constitució is open Monday to Friday 8 am to 8 pm, and Saturday 9 am to 2 pm.

ELECTRICITY

The power supply in Mallorca is: 220–225 volts.

Sockets accept two-round-pin-style plugs, so an adaptor is needed for most non-Continental appliances and a transformer for appliances operating on 100–120 volts.

TIPS/GRATUITIES

Tipping is expected for all services. As a general guide:

Yes ✓   No ✗

Restaurants (if service not included)	✓	10%
Bar service	✓	change
Tour guides	✓	1 Euro
Hairdressers	✓	change
Taxis	✓	10%
Chambermaids	✓	1 Euro
Porters	✓	1 Euro

CONSULATES

UK
☎ 971 712445

USA
☎ 971 403707

Ireland
☎ 971 722504

Australia
☎ 91 441 6025
(Madrid)

New Zealand
☎ 91 523 0228
(Madrid)

HEALTH

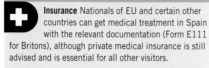
Insurance Nationals of EU and certain other countries can get medical treatment in Spain with the relevant documentation (Form E111 for Britons), although private medical insurance is still advised and is essential for all other visitors.

Dental Services Dental treatment is not usually available free of charge as all dentists practise privately. A list of *dentistas* can be found in the yellow pages of the telephone directory. Dental treatment should be covered by private medical insurance.

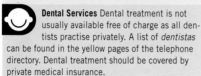
Weather The sunniest (and hottest) months are July and August with an average of 11 hours of sun each day and daytime temperatures of 29°C. Particularly during these months you should avoid the midday sun and use a strong sunblock.

Drugs Prescription and non-prescription drugs and medicines are available from pharmacies (*farmàcias*), distinguished by a large green cross. Found in towns and resorts all over the island, they are able to dispense many drugs which would be available only on prescription in other countries.

Safe Water Tap water is generally safe though it can be heavily chlorinated. Carbonated or still mineral water is cheap to buy.

CONCESSIONS

Students Holders of an International Student Identity Card may be able to obtain some concessions on travel, entrance fees, etc., but Mallorca is not really geared up for students. However, there are two youth hostels on the island, one near Palma and the other outside Alcúdia. Another cheap form of accommodation is to stay in a monastery; just turn up or book ahead.

Senior Citizens Mallorca is an excellent destination for older travellers, especially in winter when the resorts are quieter, prices more reasonable and hotels offer economical long-stay rates. The best deals are available through tour operators who specialise in holidays for senior citizens.

TRAVELLING WITH A DISABILITY

By law, all new buildings in Spain have to be equipped with wheelchair access, but many older buildings including some hotels, museums and churches are still inaccessible.

Transport facilities are generally poor, though some of Palma's buses and taxis can take wheelchairs.

The seafront promenades around the Bay of Palma are level and easily accessible, and free amphibious - wheelchairs are available for visitors with disabilities to Palma Nova and Magaluf throughout the summer.

CHILDREN

Hotels and restaurants are generally child-friendly, though facilities such as baby-changing rooms are rare.

TOILETS

There are few public toilets, so make the most of visits to museums, restaurants, cafés and bars.

LOST PROPERTY

It is important to report missing valuables to the police, if only to obtain a report for insurance purposes. If you lose your passport, contact your national embassy or consulate immediately.

Atlas

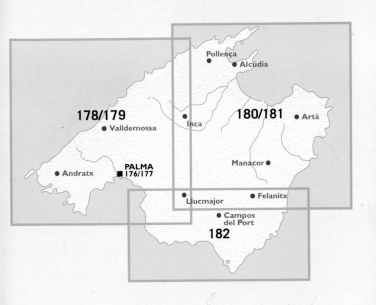

Regional Maps

0   2   4   6   8 km
0   1   2   3   4   5 miles

Motorway
Main road
Other road
Railway/Tram
□ City
▫ Town
○○ Village

■ Place of interest
✈ Airport

City Plan

0   50   100   150   200   250 metres
0   50   100   150   200   250 yards

▬ Important building
▬ Featured place of interest
▦ Steps

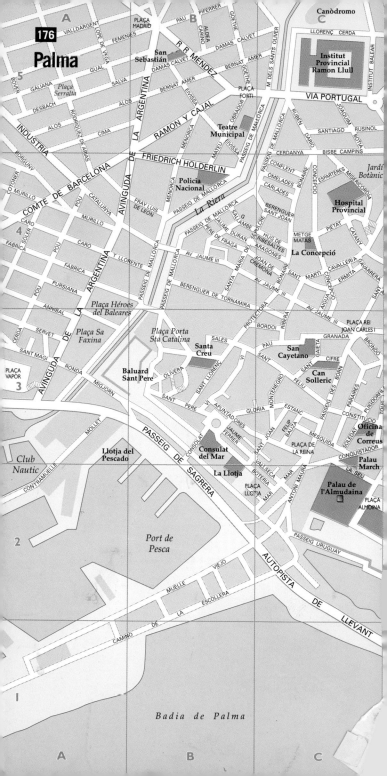

D

TESEU
VALENTI

JESUS

AV COMTE DE SALLENT

BLANQUERNA

SANTA DE MERAVELLES

REI SANC

ARXIDUC LLUIS SALVADOR

31 DE DESEMBRE

AV JUAN MARCH

E

F

CRISTINA

MARIA

REI SANC

ESTADA

EUSEBI ESTADA

5

AVINGUDA ALEMANYA

PERE DEZCALLAR

PARELLADES

PARELLADES

FRANCESC DE BORJA

JOAN LLUIS ESTELRICH

JERONI ANTIC

CECILI METEL

BARO DE PINOPAR

METEL

PLAÇA BISBE BERENGUER DE PALOU

MONTEROS

CECILI METEL

REINA ESCLARAMUNDA

MOLL

PLAÇA CONQUISTA

COMTE D'EMPURIES

SANT MIQUEL

REINA MARIA

EUSEBI ESTADA

FONTSANTA

Ferrocarriles de Mallorca

EUSEBI ESTADA

BISBE JOAN MAURA

VINYASSA

PASSEIG DE LA RAMBLA

JARDI BOTANIC

PORTA DE JESUS

OMS

SANT ELIES

MISSIO

MACANET

Hospital Militar

SANT MIQUEL

MARIE

OMS

REINA CURIE

PLAÇA D'ESPANYA

MARQUES DE LA FONTSANTA

Estació de autobúses

AV

MARGARITA CAIMARI

CAPUTXINS

ALEXANDRE

GILABERT DE CENTELLES

COSTA I LLOBERA

ROSELLO

Santa Magdalena

C DE S MAGDALENA

CARME

ANGELS

PLAÇA CARME

HORTS

MISSIO

SANT MIQUEL

P JOAN D

PLAÇA DEL OLIVAR

Santa Catalina

Mercat Olivar

PLAÇA ROSELLON

ENRIC ALZAMORA

4

La Rambla

Museu d'Art Espanyol Contemporani

PASSEIG DE LA RAMBLA

TERESES

JOSEP TOUS I FERRER

VELAZQUEZ

JOSEP ANSELM CLAVE

JAUME

SASTRE ROIG

BISBE

CAPUTXINS

FINOS

P REAL

Sant Miquel

SANT FELIP NERI

VILANOVA

Sant Jaume

OLIVA

POLS

MOLINERS

La Mercet

PLAÇA A JAUME

SINDICAT

RMENGOL

PALMA

JAQUOTOT

CAMPANER

PIVEO

GATER

SANT ESPERIT

MARTI FELIU

A DE LA MERCE

FRALES

SINDICAT

PLAÇA DE SANT ANTONI

P MANEU

LLUIS MARTI

SERINYA

Fundació la Caixa/ Gran Hotel

RIERA

Teatre Principal

SANT MIQUEL TAMORER

SANT RUBI

RUBI

VALLORI

OLI

MIRO

FERRERIA

VIDRE

SANT TANYI

PEIX CADA

GUIXERS

UNIO

PLAÇA WEYLER BERGA

PLAÇA MAJOR

SINDICAT

HOSTAL DE L'ESTEL

FLASSADERS

SOCORS

3

SANT NICOLAU

BROSSA

DANUS

Palau de Justícia

PLAÇA TAGAMENT

JAUME II

SANT BARTOMEU

MONGES

BOSSERIA

HOSTALS

LLOTGETA

ESPARTERIA

BALLESTER

ESCOLA GRADUADA

VILLA LLONGA

MAROTO

VERI

PISA

S DOMINGO

COLOM

ARGENTERIA

CARNISSERIA

SANC

CORDERIA

SAMARITANA

FARINA

PLAÇA QUARTERA

P DE TERRA SANTA

GERRERIA

ANTONI RIBAS

JERONI POU

Santa Eulàlia

SAVELLA

Palau Vivot

PLAÇA QUADRADO

P DE LLUC

S AGUSTI

RICARD ANKERMAN

Ajuntament

PLAÇA CORT

CAMPANA

PLAÇA SANTA EULALIA

C DE S FRANCESC

BOSC

BONAVENTURA

SOCORAS

Socorro

MATEU ENRIC LLADO

2

PALAU REIAL

ALMUDAINA

PLAÇA DE SANT FRANCESC

Basílica i Claustre de Sant Francesc

RAMON LLULL

ESTUDI GENERAL

Can Oleo

SANT ROC

ZANGLADA

MOREY

CRIANÇA

PLAÇA PES DE LA PALLA

PLAÇA TEMPLE

El Temple

JAUME LLUIS GARAU

GABRIEL

ALOMAR

PEREZ GALDOS

DEGANAT

Can Oleza

PONT

S CLARA

OLISAR

MONT-SION

PELLETERIA

BOTONS

TEMPLE

Sant Jeroni

ANTONI FRANCH

JOSEP ROVER MOTTA

La Seu (Catedral)

MIRAMAR

PALAU

PORTELLA

CAN SERRA

SANT ALONSO

Montesió

PLAÇA S JERONI

PLANAS I

E DE MAR

DE

Museu Diocesà

Museu de Mallorca

SEMINARI

ESCOLES

CALDERS

MONTSERRAT

SALOM

Plaça Porta d'es Camp

Banys Àrabs

DALT MURADA

Santa Clara

BASTIO D'EN BERARD

BLANQUERS

CALATRAVA

BALA ROJA

E DE SANTA FE

Ses Voltes

BASTIO DEL PRINCEP

GABRIEL DE

JOAN MARAGALL

Parc de la Mar

PASSEIG URUGUAY

AUTOPISTA DE LLEVANT

Badia de Palma

D

E

F

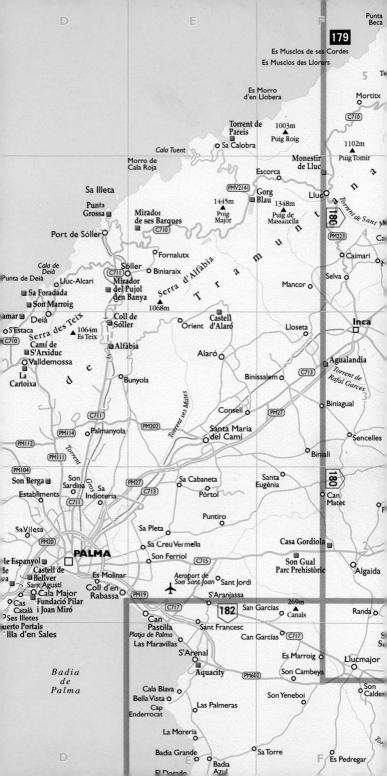

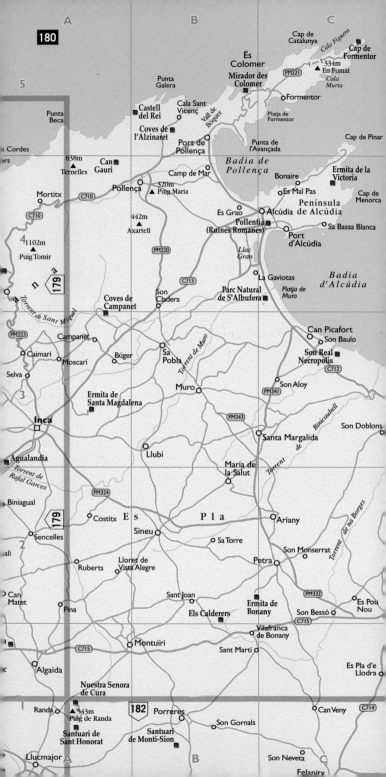

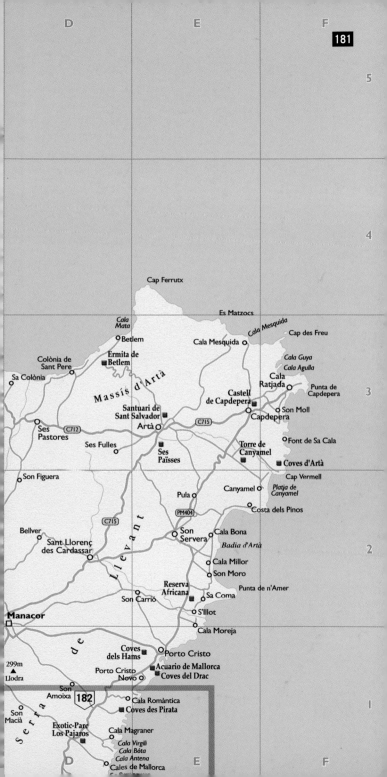

Cap Ferrutx

Es Matzocs

Cala Mata

Betlem

Cala Mesquida

Cala Mesquida   Cap des Freu

Colònia de Sant Pere

Ermita de Betlem

Cala Guya
Cala Agulla

Sa Colònia

Massís d'Artà

Cala Ratjada

Punta de Capdepera

3

Santuari de Sant Salvador

Castell de Capdepera

Son Moll

Ses Pastores

C712

Artà

C715

Capdepera

Ses Fulles

Ses Països

Torre de Canyamel

Font de Sa Cala

Coves d'Artà

Son Figuera

Cap Vermell

Pula

Canyamel

Platja de Canyamel

C715

PM404

Costa dels Pinos

Bellver

Son Servera

Cala Bona

Badia d'Artà

2

Sant Llorenç des Cardassar

Cala Millor

Son Moro

Reserva Africana

Punta de n'Amer

Son Carrió

Sa Coma

Manacor

S'Illot

Cala Moreja

Coves dels Hams

Porto Cristo

299m
Llodra

Porto Cristo Novo

Acuario de Mallorca
Coves del Drac

Son Amoixa

182

Cala Romàntica

Coves des Pirata

Son Macià

Serra de Llevant

Exotic-Parc Los Pajaros

Cala Magraner

Cala Virgili
Cala Bóta
Cala Antena

1

Cales de Mallorca

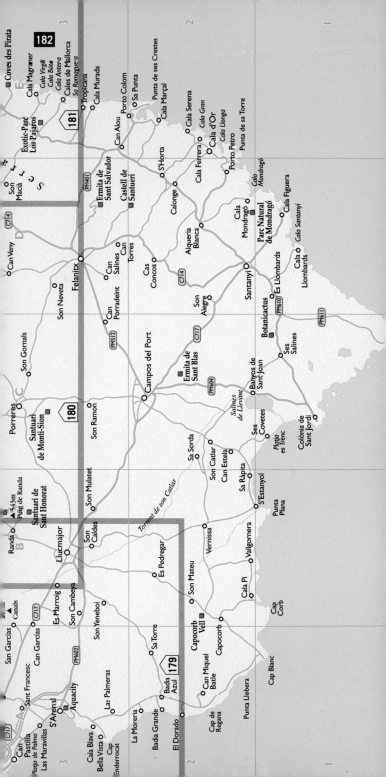

182

Coves des Pirata

Cala Magraner
Cala Virgili
Cala Bóta
Cala Antera
Cales de Mallorca
Sa Romaguera
Cala Murada
Porto Colom
Sa Punta
Punta de ses Crestes
Cala Marçal
Tropicana
Cala Serena
Cala Gran
Cala d'Or
Cala Llonga
Punta de sa Torre
Porto Petro
Cala Ferrera
Cala Mondragó
Cala Figuera
Cala Santanyí
Parc Natural de Mondragó
Cala Mondragó
Cala Llombards
Es Llombards
PM610
PM611
Botanicactus
Ses Salines
Banyos de Sant Joan
Salines de Llevant
Ses Covetes
Colònia de Sant Jordi
Platja es Trenc
Cap de Regana
Punta Llebera
Cap Blanc
Cap Corb

Coves des Pirata
Exotic-Parc Los Pajaros
181
Son Macià
C714
Can Very
Ermita de Sant Salvador
Castell de Santueri
PM401
Can Alou
S'Horta
Calonge
Alqueria Blanca
Santanyí
C714
Felanitx
Can Salines
Can Torres
Cas Concos
Son Alegre
PM512
Son Neveta
Can Porradeint
Campos del Port
PM717
Ermita de Sant Blas
PM604
Son Gormals
Son Ramon
Porreres
Santuari de Monti-Sion
180
Son Mulatet
Son Catlar
Can Estela
Sa Ràpita
S'Estanyol
Sa Sorda
Randa
543m Puig de Randa
Santuari de Sant Honorat
Son Caldes
Llucmajor
Es Pedregar
Vernissa
Vallgornera
Punta Plana
San Garcias
Canals
C717
Es Marroig
Son Cambeya
Can Garcias
PM602
Son Yeneboi
Las Palmeras
Sa Torre
Son Mateu
Cala Pi
Capocorb Vell
Capocorb
Sant Francesc
Can Pastilla
Platja de Palma
Las Maravillas
S'Arenal
Aquacity
Cala Blava
Bella Vista
Cap Enderrocat
La Morería
Badia Azul
179
Can Miquel Batle
Badia Grande
El Dorado
C717

Streetplan Index

Standard Catalan is the official language of Mallorca but the local dialect is quite different from that spoken in Barcelona. The main difference is the *article salat*, or special word for "the". In Mallorca you'll see and hear *son, sa* and *ses* instead of the standard *el, la, els* and *les* – for example *Sa Illa*, literally "The Island", referring to Mallorca itself.

Catalan pronunciation differs considerably from Spanish. Catalan is more closed and less staccato than its Castilian cousin, but like Spanish is usually phonetic, albeit with a few rules of its own, summarised below:

au	ow in wow	**ll**	lli in "million"
c	ss or k (never th)	**l.l**	ll in "silly"
ç	ss	**ny**	ni in "onion"
eu	ay-oo	**r** and **rr**	heavily rolled
g	g or j (never h)	**s**	z or ss
gu	(sometimes) w	**tx**	ch in "cheque"
h	silent	**tg/tj**	dge in "lodge"
j	j (never h)	**v**	b (*vi*, "wine", sounds like "bee")
ig at end	ch: *vaig* ("I go") sounds like "batch"	**x**	sh in "shake"

Yes / no **si / non**
OK **val/d'acord/ molt bé**
Please **si us plau**
Thank you (very much) **(moltes) gràcies**
You're welcome **de res**
Hello **hola**
Goodbye **adéu-siau**
Good morning **bon dia**
Good afternoon **bona tarda**
Good evening **bona tarda**
Goodnight **bona nit**
How are you? **com va?**
Excuse me

perdoni
How much? **quant és / val?**
I'd like... **voldria**
Open **obert**
Closed **tancat**
Today **avui**
Tomorrow **demà**
Yesterday **ahir**
Monday **dilluns**
Tuesday **dimarts**
Wednesday **dimecres**
Thursday **dijous**
Friday **divendres**
Saturday **dissabte**
Sunday **diumenge**

good **bo(na)**
bad **dolent(a)**
big **gran**
small **petit(a)**
with **amb**
without **sense**
hot **calent(a)**
cold **fred(a)**

DIRECTIONS

I'm lost **estic perdut/a**
Where is...? **on és...?**
How do I get to...? **per anar a...?**
the beach **la platja**
the telephone **el telèfon**
the toilet **els lavabos**
left **a l'esquerra**
right **a la dreta**
straight on **tot recte**
at the corner **a la cantonada**
the traffic light **al semàfor**
the crossroads **a la cruïlla**

NUMBERS

1	**un(a)**	11	**onze**	30	**trenta**	200 **dos (dues)-cents**
2	**dos (dues)**	12	**dotze**	40	**quaranta**	
3	**tres**	13	**tretze**	50	**cinquanta**	300 **tres-cents**
4	**quatre**	14	**catorze**	60	**sisanta**	400 **quatre-cents**
5	**cinc**	15	**quinze**	70	**settanta**	500 **cinc-cents**
6	**sis**	16	**setze**	80	**vuitanta**	600 **sis-cents**
7	**set**	17	**disset**	90	**nounta**	700 **set-cents**
8	**vuit**	18	**divuit**	100	**cent**	800 **vuit-cents**
9	**nou**	19	**dínou**	101	**cent un**	900 **nou-cents**
10	**deu**	20	**vint**	110	**cent deu**	1000 **mil**
		21	**vint-i-un**	120	**cent vint**	5000 **cinc mil**

MENU READER

A la plantxa grilled
Aigua water
Albergínia aubergine
All garlic
Amanida salad
Ànec duck
Anxoves anchovies
Anyell lamb
Arròs rice
Bistec steak
Bolets mushrooms
Botifarra sausage
Bou beef
Caça game
Cafè coffee
Calamar squid
Carn meat
Ceba onion
Cervesa beer
Cigrons chickpeas
Cobert cover charge
Coca cake
Col cabbage
Col-i-flor cauliflower
Conill rabbit
Cranc crab
Cru raw
Cullera spoon
Embotit sausage
Enciam lettuce
Ensaïmada Mallorcan bun
Escopinyes cockles
Farcit stuffed
Fetge liver
Fideus spaghetti
Formatge cheese
Forquilla fork
Fregit fried
Fruita fruit
Fuet salami
Gall d'indi turkey
Gambes prawns/shrimp
Ganivet knife
Gel ice
Gelat ice-cream
IVA VAT
Julivert parsley

Llagosta lobster
Llet milk
Llimona lemon
Llonganissa salami
Mantega butter
Marisc seafood
Mel honey
Mongetes beans
Muscles mussels
Oli oil
Oliva olive
Ostra oyster
Ou egg
Pa bread
Pastanaga carrot
Pastís cake
Patata potato
Pebre pepper (condiment)
Pebrot pepper (vegetable)
Peix fish
Pernil dolç ham (cooked)
Pernil serrà ham (cured)
Plàtan banana
Pollastre chicken
Poma apple
Porc pork
Postres dessert
Raïm grapes
Rap monkfish
Rostit roast
Sal salt
Salsa sauce
Salsitxa sausage
Sec dry
Sobrassada sausage paté
Sopa soup
Suc de taronja orange juice
Sucre sugar
Tonyina tuna
Truita omelette or trout
Vegetarià/na vegetarian
Vedella veal
Verdura vegetables
Vi blanc/negre white/red wine
Xai lamh
Xocolata chocolate

RESTAURANT

I'd like to book a table
Voldria reservar una taula.
A table for two, please
Una taula per a dos, si us plau.
Could we se the menu, please?
Podriem veure el menú, si us plau?
What's this? **Que és?**...
A bottle of/a glass of...
Una ampolla/copa (vas) de
Could I have the bill?
El compte, si us plau.
Service charge included
servei inclòs
Waiter/waitress **cambrer/a**
Breakfast **esmorzar**
Lunch **dinar** Dinner **sopar**
Starter **entrant** Bill **compte**
Main course **segòn plat**

ACCOMMODATION

Do you have a single/double room?
Té alguna habitació enzilla/doble?
With/without bath/toilet/shower
amb/sense bany/lavabo/dutxa
Does that include breakfast?
Inclou l'esmorzar?
Could I see the room?
Podria veure l'habitació?
I'll take this room
Ens quedarem aquesta habitació.
Thanks for your hospitality
Gràcies per la seva amabilitat.
One person **una persona**
One night **una nit**
Reservation **reserva**
Room service **servei d'habitació**
Chambermaid **cambrera**
Balcony **balcó**
Key **clau**
Lift **ascensor**
Sea view **vistes al mar**

MONEY

bank **banc**	exchange **canvi**
coin **moneda**	change **camvi**
cheque **xec**	cashier **caixer**
cheap **barat(a)**	expensive **car(a)**
shop **botiga (tenda)**	
post office **correus**	
banknote **bitllet de banc**	
travellers' cheque **xec de viatge**	
credit card **carta de crédit**	
exchange rate **tipus de canvi**	
commission charge **comissió**	
foreign currency **moneda estrangera**	

TRAVELLING

aeroplane **avió**
airport **aeroport**
train **tren**
bus **autobús**
station **estació**
boat **vaixell**
port **port**
ticket **bitllet**
single ticket **senzill-a**
return ticket **anar i tornar**
non-smoking **no fumar**
car **cotxe**
petrol **gasolina**
bus stop **la parada d'autobus**

SHOPPING

Supermarket **supermercat**
Bakery **forn (de pa)/fleca**
Self-service **autoservei**
Where can I get...? **On puc trobar...?**

Could you help me?
Em podria ajudar?
I'm looking for... **Estic buscant...**
I'm just looking **Només estic mirant, gràcies.**
It's too big/small/expensive
És massa gran/petit/car
I'll take this one
M'enduré aquest.

IF YOU NEED HELP

Help! **Ajuda!**
Could you help me, please?
Em podria ajudar, si us plau?
Do you speak English?
Parla anglès?
I don't understand **no ho entrenc**
I don't speak Catalan
No parlo català
Please could you call a doctor
quickly? **Ràpid, podria avisar a un metge, si us plau?**

INDEX

Picture credits

The Automobile Association wishes to thank the following photographers and libraries for their assistance in the preparation of this book.

ANTHONY BLAKE PHOTO LIBRARY 17 (Phototheque Culinaire), 18(t) (P Wilkins), 18(c) (Tony Robins), 19 (Tony Robins);
MICHELLE CHAPLOW 23(t), 87(b), 91, 122;
BRUCE COLEMAN COLLECTION 9(t), 9(c), 9(b), 10(t), 10(c);
JAINIE COWHAM 111;
DACS, LONDON 2000 74 L Oiseau de Proi Fonce Sur Nous (ADAGP, Paris);
JAMES DAVIS WORLDWIDE 2(l), 5, 101;
RON DAVIS/SHOOTING STAR/COLORIFIC 12;
EYE UBIQUITOUS 21(c), 69(t), 136(r);
T FISHER 51, 87(t);
GETTYONE/STONE 2(iii), 41, 46/7;
ROBERT HARDING PICTURE LIBRARY 6, 44(t), 126;
NATURE PHOTOGRAPHERS LTD 166 (P Craig-Cooper);
PICTURES COLOUR LIBRARY 21(r), 22, 116;
REX FEATURES 13(t), 13(c), 13(b);
TOPHAM PICTUREPOINT 20(c), 20(r);
G WILLIAMSON 14, 15, 16(l), 16(r), 97.

All remaining pictures are held in the Association's own library (AA PHOTO LIBRARY) and were taken by JAINIE COWHAM with the exception of the following:
P BAKER 3(v), 24, 58(b), 68(r), 88, 103, 112(r), 143, 146(t), 149, 167(l), 169, 173(bl);
K PATERSON Front & back covers (b,c,d), 2(ii), 3(l), 3(ii), 3(iii), 7, 18/9, 20/1, 21(l), 23(c), 25(c), 25(tr), 25(ctr), 25(cbr), 25(br), 26(l), 26(r), 27, 28, 29(t), 29(b), 31, 42, 44(b), 45(t), 45(b), 46, 48, 49, 50, 52, 55, 56, 57, 58(t), 66, 68(l), 69(b), 73, 74, 75, 76(t), 76(b), 83, 84, 85, 86(l), 86(r), 87(c), 89, 90, 94, 96, 99, 102, 109, 112(l), 113(t), 113(b), 117, 119, 123, 124, 124/5, 133, 136(l), 137(b), 139, 140/1, 144, 145, 146(b), 148, 159, 160, 161, 165, 168, 173(t), 173(br);
J TIMS Front cover (a).

Key for terms appearing above: (t) top; (b) bottom; (r) right; (c) centre.

Acknowledgements

Carol Baker would like to express her heartfelt gratitude to the Rabassa family of Pollenç for 30 years of gracious guidance, friendship and hospitality.

Questionnaire

Dear Traveller
Your comments, opinions and recommendations are very important to us. So please help us to improve our travel guides by taking a few minutes to complete this simple questionnaire.

You do not need a stamp (unless posted outside the UK). If you do not want to remove this page from your guide, then photocopy it or write your answers on a plain sheet of paper.

Send to: The Editor, Spiral Guides, AA World Travel Guides, FREEPOST SCE 4598, Basingstoke RG21 4GY.

Your recommendations...
We always encourage readers' recommendations for restaurants, night-life or shopping – if your recommendation is used in the next edition of the guide, we will send you a FREE AA Spiral Guide of your choice. Please state below the establishment name, location and your reasons for recommending it.

_____

_____

_____

_____

_____

Please send me AA Spiral _____
(see list of titles inside the back cover)

About this guide...
Which title did you buy?

_____ **AA Spiral**

Where did you buy it? _____

When? m m / y y

Why did you choose an AA Spiral Guide? _____

_____

_____

_____

_____

Did this guide meet your expectations?

Exceeded ☐   Met all ☐   Met most ☐   Fell below ☐

Please give your reasons _____

_____

_____

_____

_____

continued on next page...

Were there any aspects of this guide that you particularly liked?

_____
_____
_____
_____
_____
_____

Is there anything we could have done better?

_____
_____
_____
_____
_____
_____
_____

About you...

Name (Mr/Mrs/Ms) _____

Address _____

_____

_____ Postcode _____

Daytime tel nos _____

Which age group are you in?

Under 25 ☐   25–34 ☐   35–44 ☐   45–54 ☐   55–64 ☐   65+ ☐

How many trips do you make a year?

Less than one ☐   One ☐   Two ☐   Three or more ☐

Are you an AA member? Yes ☐   No ☐

About your trip...

When did you book? mm/ y y   When did you travel? mm/ y y

How long did you stay? _____

Was it for business or leisure? _____

Did you buy any other travel guides for your trip?   ☐ Yes   ☐ No

If yes, which ones? _____
_____

Thank you for taking the time to complete this questionnaire. Please send it to us as soon as possible, and remember, you do not need a stamp (unless posted outside the UK).